The Trust Factor

7 Strategies To Convert Your Online Visitors Into Lifetime Customers

_____

Garrett Pierson & Scott Brandley

The Trust Factor

First published in 2011 by Outstanding Ventures.
Copyright © 2011 by Garrett Paul Pierson and David Scott Brandley.

ISBN 978-0-615-56027-4

Printed in the United States of America

10 9 8 7 6 5 4 3 2 1

Contents

Chapter 1

Thinking Big

Do you remember your very first business idea?

I remember mine. It all started at my grandpa's kitchen table one lazy summer day.

My Uncle Luke and I were young, scrawny 14 year-olds with nothing but free time and big dreams. On that particular day we came up with a brilliant idea for a brand new lawn mowing business called Quick Blades. We thought it was the coolest lawn mowing company name EVER! In fact, it was so good that we couldn't even *think* of another name.

That magical afternoon, Luke and I spent several hours planning out how we were going to become the richest kids in our schools. We came up with marketing tools that consisted of a really cool logo, some stylish uniform sketches and several hand-drawn fliers. We also created what we thought was a brilliant franchising plan.

You see, because Luke and I lived in different cities, we had to create a system that would work for both of us. So we had the genius idea of recruiting other teenagers as franchisees. In a nutshell, they would do all of their own marketing, mowing, trimming, and collecting, and then they would give us a share of the profits for the rights to our super cool logo, our fliers, uniforms, and a rudimentary, top secret formula that we had devised for determining how much to charge for each lawn they serviced.

Interestingly enough, there was a very important, underlying concept that we understood, even back then.
It was this...

Building strong 'Relationships of Trust' with customers is the key to long-term business success.

You see, even as nerdy 14 year old kids, we realized that if we could get someone to trust us enough to let us mow their lawn just once, and if we did a really good job, then there was a really good chance that they would let us mow their lawn every week from that point on.

This was how Luke and I were going to get rich. By building a group of loyal, lifetime customers, we believed that we could ultimately create long-term, stable recurring revenue. And although Quick Blades didn't pan out exactly as we had hoped, twenty years later we are successfully executing this important concept in all our various businesses.

It's timeless. It's proven. And it works!

Over the last 14 years of doing business, we have sold millions of dollars of products and services online. During that time, we have discovered that trust is one of the most powerful assets that a website owner can have. In fact, trust is such a crucial, integral part of our business that we literally felt compelled to write this book, which is a compilation of seven of the most effective ways that we've discovered to build trust with visitors and potential prospects and convert them into long-lasting, loyal, repeat customers.

One of the first things you will realize is that this book doesn't follow a traditional format.

For starters, this book is written by myself (Scott Brandley) and Garrett Pierson. We have both collaborated on each chapter. However, I have written the majority of certain chapters while Garrett has written the majority of others.

Sometimes Garrett or I share a personal story, and at other times we will discuss shared experiences that have taught us important business principles. We've also thrown in some of our favorite quotes and sayings and we've both integrated our various backgrounds and expertise on different subjects.

Ultimately, we feel that the unique set up and writing style of the book make it attractive and entertaining, as we emphasize important ideas and concepts that will help you in your business.

Why you should listen to us:

If you have a website and you sell products or services online, then the information you read in this book will help you take your business to the next level. Garrett and I have nearly 20 years of combined internet experience, which you can instantly and easily leverage.

What kind of experience? Well, for me it all started waaaay back in 1997. (You know, back when Al Gore invented the Internet.) In those days email was all the craze and online shopping was so new that many shopping carts didn't even have SSL certificates (a commonly-used security mechanism on the internet.) In a short amount of time, my dad and I figured out how to create a web page and post drawings with a handful of printed t-shirt designs on it. Before we knew it, we were in business.

I wish I had taken a picture of that first site. It was painfully ugly. But somehow, after only a few days, we actually got an order! I was so excited that I ran around the house jumping and screaming like I was possessed! It was great. I'll never forget it.

Over time, the orders increased. We went from getting an order a week, to an order a day, to 3 orders a day, to 10 orders a day and it just kept going up. Before long, we had dominated the search engines. We were even beating out huge brick and mortar stores that had been in the industry for decades! The great thing was that it was just me and my dad in a condo basement. Talk about leveling the playing field!

After a few years, we had grown to the point where we were maxing out our niche online. It was at that point that we decided to sell our online clothing company.

Ultimately, we sold the business because we realized two things:

The first thing we realized was that selling physical products online is hard work. If you sell products online, you can probably relate. Selling products involves inventory, suppliers, sorting, packaging, shipping, out-of-stock items, returns, small profit margins, and a long list of other challenges. Long story short, we decided that we didn't want to sell products anymore.

Now don't get me wrong. Millions of people sell products online every day. And although we were very good at it, it just wasn't for us long-term.

The second thing we realized was that we loved helping other people succeed online. We also discovered that we had a special skill for developing software, so we decided to create valuable, innovative digital solutions and services to help online business owners become more successful.

This was about the time that Garrett and I crossed paths.

Prior to my meeting Garrett, he was in the health care industry. Back In 2004, Garrett was given a very unique opportunity to build a health care company from scratch. With only two people, an office and two laptops, in a few short years they created a multi-million dollar health care company with hundreds of employees, therapists and nurses.

Once the company was up and running smoothly, Garrett was asked to go in and turn around a large assisted living community that had been neglected and abused by several years of bad management. This new assignment took him away from his family and left him with many nights with nothing to do. It was during these nights that Garrett started learning all he could about Online Marketing, Search Engine Optimization and Social

Media. It didn't take long before he had become a online marketing expert, attracting the attention of several prominent marketers like Alex Mandossian, Russell Brunson, and Joel Comm, just to name a few. Since then, Garrett has been invited to speak at several different events throughout the country teaching many of the strategies that will be taught in this book.

With his new found passion to help teach website owners about SEO and social media marketing, it wasn't long before Garrett left the health care industry and moved back home to Utah. We became acquainted shortly after that and ever since then Garrett and I have worked together, creating and developing innovative online services to help website owners become more successful.

One way we achieve this is through our 'Outstanding Ventures' email list – a special email newsletter that goes out to tens of thousands of like-minded website owners throughout the world; discussing the latest marketing techniques and trust-building strategies.

Do you have 'The Trust Factor'?

Ultimately, running a successful online business boils down to three main things:

- having a valuable product or service
- generating traffic (prospects), and
- consistently building long-lasting relationships with your customers.

If you get these three things right, everything else will naturally fall into place and you will have a very good chance of being successful online.

It all comes back to what I inherently knew when I was a kid with the Quick Blades lawn mowing idea. That formula for success that I knew back then is the exact same formula that our company is using to make millions online, and it will be the exact same formula that we use 5, 10, even 20 years from now.

What's your score? - www.TrustFactorBook.com/score

To help you get off to a running start, Garrett and I have put together the 7 core trust strategies that will help you convert your online visitors into lifetime customers. These 7 strategies cover everything from how your customers perceive your website design, to how they contact you, to how safe they feel buying from you, to the social proof you integrate into your website.

Each of these 7 strategies build on each other throughout the book, creating a powerful synergistic effect that help entice and motivate your customers to buy from you and to keep coming back.

Who needs this book? You do, if you are:

- A website owner who sells (or plans to sell) a product or service online
- An entrepreneur that is wanting to start a business in today's market
- A brick and mortar store that wants to take their business online
- An affiliate marketer that promotes others products or services
- A webmaster or designer that services clients
- A business coach or teacher that helps companies grow

No matter where you currently happen to be, you will have the opportunity to take what we teach and apply it to your business instantly. In fact, nothing that we are going to teach you is revolutionary (as much as we would like it to be). Successful online companies are already using many of these strategies. This book compiles them in a strategic manner that will help you implement them quickly and effectively.

The purpose of this book is to arm you with tools that will help you become the "go to" company or service in your market. By following our advice, you will outperform your competition in every trust aspect of your business. Think of this book as the ammunition you need to survive in this jungle we call the internet. It doesn't matter if you are just starting out or have been running a business for 40 years. These strategies will protect and serve you well in all cases.

The Game has changed!

It's pretty obvious that doing business has changed dramatically over the last five, even ten years. This change is not a bad thing, in fact it's a great opportunity for all of us to put on our thinking caps and reinvent how business is done. Online consumers are more educated and demanding than ever. It is time to give them exactly what they want and desire. What is that precisely, you might be asking? Well, that is what you will learn in the pages that follow.

Here are some suggestions we have while reading this book:

1. Don't skip any chapters - even if you think you are already applying a certain strategy. Make sure you read the entire chapter to ensure that you haven't missed something important.

2. Keep in mind that not everything will apply to you. You may find something that we are teaching may not fit your niche or business. This is totally fine. Try and see the big picture. For example, you might think, "I can't use this idea, but how many of my customers, employees, or vendors could use it?" Keeping this frame of mind will improve relationships with those involved in making you successful.

3. Share this book with others. If you have business partners, give them the opportunity to read this book so that you can all be on the same page when making changes to your business. In addition, make sure you share what you learn with friends and colleagues that have a business as well.

What's your score? - www.TrustFactorBook.com/score

4. Apply what you learn. The only way that you will truly succeed in anything is if you consistently apply these principles. We are going to be sharing with you some important strategies that can literally change your life and the direction of your business - but only if you apply them. We suggest that you read a chapter, apply what you have learned, then go to the next chapter. This will help you be more productive and efficient.

Very few people actually understand the complexities of running a business with this relatively new medium called the Internet. However, by the time you finish this book, you will truly grasp the importance of TRUST and you'll know more than 99% of today's online business owners.

Our entire goal of this book is to help and teach you. If for whatever reason you are not quite understanding or following our points and examples, feel free to contact us anytime. You can reach us by email at questions@trustfactorbook.com. And to be super transparent, here is our phone number: 801-334-7078. Just ask for Scott or Garrett!

So without further delay, let's jump right into Trust Factor #1.

Chapter 2

Perception is Reality

Ice cream. Everybody loves it.

In fact, it's so popular that every day vendors across the world drive all around cities and towns, selling it out of their trucks and vans.

So, let me ask you a question. Let's pretend for a moment that the two ice cream vans below sold the exact same type of ice cream. If both of these vans drove through your neighborhood, which one are you more likely to buy ice cream from?

If your experience has been anything like mine, you've probably seen your fair share of dilapidated ice cream vans like the van on the left, driving uncomfortably slow down your street. My kids are constantly begging me to buy ice cream from them but I usually refuse to do so because the vans always look so shady.

But here's the interesting thing. I would let them buy an ice cream from the van on the right without hesitation. Why? Because it looks trustworthy.

That's TRUST Factor #1 - Perception is Reality.

What's your score? - www.TrustFactorBook.com/score

You see, our lives are based on our own individual view of reality - how we see the world. It doesn't matter if our perception is based on fact or fiction; we still base our decisions on it.

For example, my wife hates roller coasters and thrill rides where she feels like she is not in control. Why? Because when she was about four years old, her mother took her on the Matterhorn at Disneyland and proceeded to scream bloody murder the whole time as if they were both going to die. She permanently traumatized my wife and changed her perception of what it was like to be out of control. This perception was further ingrained every time her mother would retell the story of their 'near-death' roller coaster experience and how she should have never taken her helpless four-year old on that ride. (Just for the record, I love my mother-in-law. She just made a mistake that had unintended consequences.)

Contrast that with my children's experience. I love roller coasters. So when my kids were young I would tell them that as soon as they turned five, I was going to take them on the roller coaster with me. They were so excited! I knew that the first roller coaster ride would make all the difference, so I made sure to play it up all the way onto the ride, during the ride, and especially as soon as the ride was over.

I remember looking at my kids as they got off their first roller coaster; their little bodies shaking from the adrenaline, still in shock. Intentionally, I would totally play it up, saying things like "Wasn't that awesome? Remember how exciting it was when we suddenly dropped down and then went through the loopty-loops? Let's do it again!" I intentionally fed them with positive reinforcement because I wanted them to love roller coasters as much as I do. And it worked! My kids love roller coasters and they beg me every year to take them to the amusement park.

Isn't it interesting how we can influence people's decisions and their perception of reality? The truth is that our perceptions are constantly changing. Every time we experience something new like read a book, watch the news, or talk to a friend, spouse, or co-worker, we affect our reality.

Here are some other real-world examples of how perception affects our reality...

- Chainsaws at spook alleys. We all know that there isn't a chain on the chainsaw, but it's still as scary as hell.

- Superstitions. Have you ever had a friend who never washes his lucky basketball socks? Do you know someone that goes through a specific ritual every time his team plays away games?

- Groups at school. Have you ever dreaded being asked to get into groups because you thought that nobody would want to be in your group?

- Diamond rings. Why is it that somehow our love for our wives is directly proportionate to the size of diamond ring we buy her?

- Bad neighborhoods. Do you avoid driving in particular neighborhoods because you heard rumors or stories about it, or because it appeared to be run down?

The point here is that our entire lives are built around perception. Here's another example that directly relates to your business.

- Buying online. Have you ever decided to not buy a product from a particular website because the site didn't look credible, and then bought it from another website that did? Just like the ice cream vans, people are much more likely to buy from a website that looks professional, credible, and trustworthy over one that doesn't appear to have these characteristics.

Did you notice how I used the word "looks" both times I mentioned the ice cream truck example?

What's your score? - www.TrustFactorBook.com/score

The interesting thing about perception and trust is that something only has to "look" or appear trustworthy in order for people to initially trust it.

Fortunately, in the case of most businesses, those that look credible usually are, but not always.

There are cases where a website can look like a million bucks and yet have an ineffective or low grade product, or even worse, be a scam. If you want to see an example of this, just type in the term HYIP in Google and see what comes up. HYIP stands for High Yield Investment Program and every single one of them are ponzi schemes (warning: if you do a search for HYIP in Google, please don't get sucked in. They can be very compelling.) Unfortunately, the people behind them are getting so good at making their sites look credible and professional that they can deceive even the most conservative, careful investors.

To prove my point, even I got tempted to sign up for an HYIP when I was doing research on this chapter. I clicked on a HYIP ad in Google that showed a 45% ROI per year, (which is on the low end for what many of them claim) and as soon as the website loaded, it had Yahoo Finance logos, it talked about the FDIC, the FOREX market, truth in savings disclosures - the works. My spider senses were tingling, telling me to run, but it looked so compelling that I had a hard time leaving the site. I think it's human nature to try to get something for nothing. Unfortunately it rarely ever works out to our benefit. This is just another example of how our perception can affect our reality.

Okay, I've got one more really good example before I drive the point home.

Do you drink bottled water? Statistically, the average American drinks 167 single-use plastic water bottles each year, 86% of which go directly into landfills. So why do we drink bottled water? Because it's healthier than tap water, right? That's what most people would tell you.

The reality is that this generally isn't the case - especially in the US. In fact, several studies have been done and in many cases tap water is just as safe as bottled water. Ironically, several of the larger bottled water brands are nothing more than treated municipal tap water. Even in New York City, the water is just as clean as bottled water.

Case in point, back in 2005, 20/20 did a segment on bottled water. They took a sample from a drinking fountain in the middle of New York and compared it to five major bottled water brands, namely Evian (from France), Aquafina, Iceland Spring (from Iceland), Poland Spring, and American Fare (Kmart's low cost brand), and when the results came back, there was no difference in water quality between the bottled water and water from the drinking fountain.

Okay, so if bottled water isn't any healthier, maybe we drink it because it tastes better? We'll 20/20 thought the same thing, so they took it even one step further and did a blind taste test. Surprisingly, the cheap American Fare Kmart brand won, followed by Aquafina (aka 'filtered' tap water), followed by a tie between Iceland Spring and the actual NYC tap water. Fourth place went to Poland Spring, and the expensive, French Evian came in dead last with half of the taste testers saying that it tasted bad.

My point in all of these examples is simply this; we **all make decisions based on how we perceive reality.** We go to specific restaurants over others because we perceive one to be better than the other. We buy organic fruit because we perceive it to be better than non-organic fruit. We buy bottled water because we perceive it to be healthier and better tasting than regular tap water.

The reality is that reality doesn't really matter.

That is your ace in the hole as a website owner. The Internet gives you the ability to be whoever you want to be. I mean, who would have thought that two guys in a condo basement would end up directly competing against multi-million dollar brick and mortar stores that had been established for years, but we did, and the great thing about the Internet is that you can too.

The key is to make your website look credible, professional, and trustworthy. The best way to do that is by benchmarking.

Benchmarking is one of the few concepts I learned in university that I have actually been able to apply to the real business world. If you've never heard of the term before, here's the stuffy BusinessDictionary.com definition: (yawn)...

> "Benchmarking is a measurement of the quality of an organization's policies, products, programs, strategies, etc., and their comparison with standard measurements, or similar measurements of its peers.

> The objectives of benchmarking are (1) to determine what and where improvements are called for, (2) to analyze how other organizations achieve their high performance levels, and (3) to use this information to improve performance."

And now here's our version of benchmarking:

> "Benchmarking is the process of researching your competitors and making a list of all of the things they do better or different than you, and then brainstorming ways that you can improve upon what they're doing in order to give your business a competitive edge, while providing your customers with the best overall product or service in the market."

Every time we create a new product or service in our company, we go through this process, not only in terms of the actual product or service but in site design as well. We gather ideas from several of the top companies from the market we are entering. By combining several of the benchmarks we've collected along with our own unique ideas, we end up with a product or service that is vastly different and far better than anything else on the market.

Benchmarking can improve many areas of your business. Hopefully you are considering several ways to put this concept into practice. For the purposes of this chapter, however, let's focus on benchmarking your website design.

One of the main benefits of benchmarking the most successful website designs in your market is that these companies are already successful, which means they're most likely doing more things right than they are doing wrong. By looking at how these competing websites display information to their customers, it will help spark ideas on ways that you can customize and even improve upon your existing website design that you might not have considered.

One thing I want to stress is that benchmarking is not copying. Do not copy what your competitors are doing. The whole purpose of benchmarking is to find out what's already working and then internalize it, improve it, and make it your own.

In today's market you have to be authentic. If you're not, people will see right through your website, your marketing and even your product. Being real and true to who you are as a person and as a company is key when using benchmarking as a tool.

Bottom line; if you're going to sell to a market where there are already well-established, multi-million dollar companies, then you need to look like a multi-million dollar company, and you do that by benchmarking. That way, when potential customers visit both your website and your multi-million dollar competitor's websites, they won't know the difference. In other words, in their reality, they will perceive both you and your competitors as equals.

Remember - Perception is Reality.

What's your score? - www.TrustFactorBook.com/score

A word of Caution: Always tell the truth.

As tempting as it may be to slightly enhance the benefits, features, or test results of your product or service, or add a fake testimonial or two in order to make things sound more appealing, don't do it. Online shoppers are always on the defensive, and anything that looks slightly off or too good to be true can quickly throw up red flags.

Your reputation online is essential to your success, so you need to be careful to always keep yourself and your business practices above reproach. If not, it is very easy for an untrusting or disillusioned customer to make a damaging post about your website to a third party complaint site or social network that can permanently harm your reputation.

Another reason why it's so important for your site to look as credible and trustworthy as possible is because the search engines are continuously improving, and are moving more and more toward visual results, like images and video, instead of text.

Let's take Google for example. Starting in 2011, whenever you do a search, they display an instant preview next to each result. If you happen to click on any of the instant preview links, an instant snapshot of that website's homepage will pop up on the screen, like the one on the following page.

Whether you realize it or not, this little feature is a game changer. Suddenly people don't have to wade through 10 different titles and page descriptions before deciding which site to visit. Suddenly they don't have to click on all 10 search results to see what each site has to offer. Now they don't even have to go to the website to see which websites appear to be the most credible, professional, and trustworthy. They can view your website and all of your competitor's sites side-by-side in seconds, right from the Google search engine.

Now more than ever, having a good, solid website design is vital to your online success.

Fortunately, everything you need to make your website look absolutely amazing is relatively inexpensive and right at your fingertips, thanks to online freelancing.

Online freelancing is a wonderful resource that puts thousands of professionals at your beck and call 24/7. Anything you can imagine or need, you can find a freelancer to do it for you at a very reasonable rate. Just go to one of several freelancing sites online, post your job description, push send, and within a few minutes, freelancers from all over the world will start bidding on your job.

Once you've got several bids, you can go through their resumes, portfolios or chat with them directly. Haggle and look at what their previous customers had to say. Because website owners have thousands of freelance workers to choose from, the cost for getting quality work done is very inexpensive. Once you have decided on a particular freelancer, you award him the bid and he will start working on your project.

Here are a few things we've learned over the years that will help you have the best freelance experience possible.

1. Make sure they speak English <u>fluently</u>. We tend to hire more people from countries where English is their primary language, even if we have to pay more. There just seems to be a huge disconnect otherwise and it can take a lot longer to get things done.

2. Make sure they agree to unlimited revisions. You want to make sure that they will keep making changes to their work until you are completely satisfied.

3. Don't pay them all of the money upfront. Hold at least half of it until the job is done and you are satisfied with the results.

4. Don't choose the cheapest bid for your job unless their resume, portfolio and English are amazing. Often times, these people are freelancers who got bad ratings from a previous job and so they created a new profile. There are obviously exceptions, so just make sure you do your homework.

5. Give them as much direction as you can in your job post. We often refer to specific websites that we like and tell them to "make me a menu like this style," or "create two columns like

this website." Basically, the more information you can give them upfront, the smoother the project will go.

One final word of advice. While it's tempting to try and do everything yourself - especially when you're starting out, one of the best things you can do is to let other people that are experts in their fields do the things that they do best.

Don't try to learn php.
Don't try to learn html.
Don't try to learn graphic design.
Don't try to learn professional photography.

All of these things can be outsourced online by freelance experts for very reasonable prices. However, the one thing I advise you is

DO become experienced at hiring and managing freelancers.

If you can successfully hire and manage freelancers, then you can do anything you could ever dream of online. Once you know how to effectively leverage online freelancers, you can say to your friends "I've got people for that" and actually mean it.

Some of our favorite freelance sites are Elance.com, Scriptlance.com and Guru.com.

You don't have to use a freelancer for everything. If you are ready to hire part-time or full-time employees then you can leverage their time and expertise to help you instead of or in addition to freelancers.

For example, we currently have two graphic designers, two programmers and two customer service representatives that all work directly in our office. Although we still use freelancers on a regular basis, this core group of staff gives us certain freedoms and flexibilities that we currently need in our business.

What's your score? - www.TrustFactorBook.com/score

If you're just starting out, it's a good idea to rely more heavily on freelancing. Then, once you're established and growing, odds are that you'll find a mix between freelancing and in-house staff that work well for you.

In closing, we hope you always remember that perception is reality. The way your website looks will make or break your business online. There are literally billions of web pages out there on the World Wide Web. Your content and your design must stand out above the rest for you to become the authority and the "Go To" place for consumers in your market.

Also keep in mind that change is a good thing. We are constantly updating and improving our websites - sometimes on a monthly basis. This doesn't mean that you have to change this often. But it does mean that you need to constantly be looking for ways to improve the perception you are portraying.

On that note, may your ice cream be delicious and unique, and may your ice cream truck always look like a million bucks!

Chapter 3

The Art of Transparency

It was October 1st, just two weeks away from Mary's fortieth birthday. Her husband was taking her to Hawaii and she wanted a new swimsuit for the trip, so she decided to buy one online.

She had never purchased anything online before, so buying a swimsuit without being able to try it on was a big leap of faith. Still, all her friends were buying clothing online and so she decided to give it a try. Her first stop was Google. She typed in the keywords "women's swimsuit" and started browsing the results.

The first website she came across on the list was a company that she had never heard of. She clicked on the link and before long she had found the perfect swimsuit. Then her fears of finding the right one forced her to look for a phone number to call about sizing. She couldn't find a number anywhere on the website. Even though it was the perfect suit, she hesitantly went back to the search engine to find another website. She wasn't going to risk getting the wrong size.

She clicked on the second website on the list. As luck would have it, she found the same swimsuit! The price was competitive and the site gave her several ways for her to contact them including chat, email, and phone.

With the click of a button, Mary was chatting with a service representative who answered all her questions. Unlike her experience with the first website, she felt comfortable with this website and placed her order right away. Just to make sure that her order went through correctly, she called the toll-free support phone number. The customer service representative that answered her call confirmed that everything was correct and that her order would be shipped out that day.

With the story above, you've probably guessed that this chapter is going to be about customer service. No, we're not going to rave on about how some companies are great and others aren't. What we are going to do is give you simple steps on how to show customers that you care. Hopefully you do.

Let's go back and break down Mary's experience.

Like everyone does at one point or another, Mary was making a purchase online for the first time. But whether it's someone's first or five-hundredth time buying online, as a website owner, your first priority is to help your prospects become loyal, happy paying customers. A proven way to do this is by making them feel all warm and fuzzy inside while they are visiting and internalizing your website.

So you might be asking, "How do I help the visitor feel all warm and fuzzy?" Great question.

You must be transparent.

You can't hide behind your computer and run a successful online business anymore. People need to know that you are a legitimate company and that you can be trusted. Transparency is not only essential for improving customer service; it is quickly becoming the expectation.

Here are five important methods of transparency that will help you gain your customers' trust – giving you a substantial advantage in your marketplace.

1. Toll Free Phone Number

2. Email with Customer Support Ticketing System

3. Live Chat

4. Physical Address

5. Social Media

We'll break these down as to how, why and what you should be doing with each of the five strategies. But before we do, try answering this question.

What percentage of online shoppers do you think want access to an email, a phone number, and a physical address?

For years we posted a statistic on one of our websites from a Consumer Reports 'WebWatch' national survey of online shoppers. In that survey 81% of the people polled said that having access to a website's email address, street address and phone number was 'very important' to them.

That's right. 81% want to know how they can get a hold of you by email, phone, or an address, even though most of them never will. People need to feel that they are going to be treated like a human and not a number. They need to know that you care. You can show them you do by being TRANSPARENT.

1 – Toll Free Phone Number

It is easier than ever to get your own toll free phone number. Not only is it easy, it is now incredibly affordable. The purpose of having a toll free phone number is to give the impression that you are a stable and legitimate business. We also suggest you get a PBX associated with your toll free number. What is a PBX? PBX stands for Private Branch Exchange. It's an automated answering system. When someone calls, the machine will say something like "Hi, welcome to…, click one for sales, click two for support..."

This makes you look bigger than you are and gives you the ability to help online consumers feel safe about doing business with you. Here's the key with using a PBX and toll free phone number; ANSWER THE PHONE!

What's your score? - www.TrustFactorBook.com/score

Don't just get a PBX or toll free number and think that it is going to help you make more sales. You're only going to succeed if you actually answer the phone and help the person with their question or problem.

We use and suggest RingCentral.com for your toll free and PBX services. If you just simply want a toll free number, we recommend Kall8.com. Both services are great and affordable.

Do you have to get a toll free number? No. If you are a local business where the only people that order from you live in your local geographic area, the best thing to do is to use your local phone number with the area code.

The next strategy is to make sure that you have your phone number visible and easy to find on your website. This means that it needs to be on all pages either in the header, footer or sidebar. Many people ask us which is better and the answer is that every website and market is different. It is something that you will have to test. The key is just making sure that you have the phone number on all your pages and that you actually answer the phone (highly recommended) or at least have voice mail and return the calls in a timely manner (not recommended).

2 – Email (Ticketing System)

This seems like a no brainer, but you would be surprised at how many websites miss this essential step. Giving your customers and potential customers a way to email you is the only way that you will take your business to the next level. This is simply another channel that you can provide for your visitors or existing customers to access your customer service team (even if it is only you).

Here are three ways that you can fulfill this step to transparency:

Email address – simply add your email address somewhere on your website so that people can copy and paste it into their email client. Just like the phone number, make sure that people can easily find your email address. What most people are used to is a link or image that says "Contact Us."

Contact Form (better option) – Create a contact form that people can fill out and that will forward to your email address after they click submit. If you don't know how to do this yourself you can find a programmer on Elance.com to help you. This gives your visitors an easy way to quickly contact you without having to copy and paste your email address to email you.

Ticket System (best option) – Invest in a service that gives you a web-based ticket system that keeps all your visitor and customer questions in a safe and organized place. This option, like the PBX option in step one allows you to look much larger, more established and more professional. Here are some of the top support software ticket systems out there – Rhino Support, Zendesk, Kayako, and Assistly.

3- Live Chat

When we added Live Chat to our customer service options, we noticed a big increase in sales and customer satisfaction. Remember Mary's story? She was able to quickly get her questions answered by a customer representative via Live Chat. This was exactly what Mary needed to break the ice, create a relationship of trust, and make her first purchase online.

This is one of our favorite ways of thrashing the competition, by simply adding Live Chat. Some companies try and copy our products and services. They usually do a very poor job because they don't implement the small, important things that make a difference, like Live Chat.

The biggest concern with Live Chat is that there always has to be someone available to man it. If you are going to use Live Chat then yes, you will have to either man it yourself or hire someone to take care of all the chats. But if you really want to make a difference while selling more and retaining more customers, then you have do what larger, established companies do in order to put your company on the same level, and one of those things is Live Chat.

That being said, there is a trick that we have implemented with Live Chat that has worked well for us. When our customer service team comes in to work in the morning, they log in to our Live Chat for all of our businesses. As soon as they log in, the Live Chat buttons on our websites instantly turn on. And whenever they log out, the Live Chat button simply disappears.

We never use a 'Live Chat is Offline' button. We believe that you should tell people what you can do, not what you can't. If we are offline, new visitors have no idea that we even offer Live Chat because it is only available when someone is available to man it.

Here is how we do this.

Most Live Chat systems give you the ability to create an Online image and an Offline image. So again, if you are logged in to chat, the Online image is displayed on your website. Then the trick is to make your Offline image a 1 pixel transparent image. What this does is when you are logged off of chat the image changes to the 1 pixel image that is not visible. The idea is to be logged on to chat as much as possible. But when you're logged off, at least this way you are not saying, "Hey, we're not here." The visitor can then use one of your other passive channels to contact you.

This idea of running Live Chat allows you to be there when you can, and if you're not there, you don't have to look unavailable. Don't you hate it when you go to a website that has live chat that always says "Live Chat Offline?" Not cool!

You're probably wondering where you can go to get an affordable Live Chat service. There are many options out there. We recommend you find a system that gives you the ability to have a ticket system and Live Chat together, that you can manage all in one place.

Once again, Rhino Support, Zendesk, Kayako, and Assistly all give you a support ticket system along with Live Chat, although some are more expensive than others. Choose which will work best for you and your business.

Here's another tip that has worked well for us. When choosing a support system and Live Chat service, make sure that you choose one that is simple and not packed full of unnecessary features that you will never use. These systems can take additional time to load and often require a two-three week learning curve. Keep it simple. It's easy to get overwhelmed if there are too many options.

You should place your Live Chat images or links at the top of your website pages. Ideally, you should have the image or link on all pages, but especially on your home page and product pages.

4 – Physical Address

When we teach this concept, we often get resistance - especially from those who are just starting their online business. Why? Because people don't like to put their physical address on their website. They worry about people coming to their house or office. But the truth is, that unless you service a specific local area, no one will ever come to your house or office. Besides, if someone ever did come to your house or office, wouldn't you welcome him or her in and help them out?

So here is your next step to transparency and TRUST…

…Put your physical address on your website!

Place the address in the footer or on your 'Contact Us' page. Just make sure that you place it where online shoppers can see it.

Why is this so important? People need to know that you are a real business. Because you are willing to put your address on your website, visitors will have more confidence and TRUST in you and your company.

WARNING! Do not use a PO Box if at all possible. Think about it. If you go to a website and all they have is a PO Box listed, that immediately throws up red flags. It says, "We are too worried about you finding us to give you our physical address." Customers know that websites that are not transparent cannot be trusted. By not displaying your address it may appear that you have something to hide.

We know there are some exceptions when it comes to using a physical address. For example, if you are a celebrity or have a product or service that requires a high level of security or anonymity. The rest of us, however, need to implement this simple but effective strategy for building TRUST.

5 – Social Media

Large corporations are now utilizing social media as a platform for providing customer service. Companies like Comcast, Dell, Jet Blue, and Home Depot are benefiting from this powerful, yet relatively new method of servicing customers.

Take Comcast for example. They use Twitter at http://twitter.com/comcastcares to help customers that are frustrated or have questions. They even have Bill Gerth (Comcastbill) as the face of their Twitter presence. The company answers questions, helps customers and tries to make things right. Do they always succeed in making everyone happy? Not likely. But at least they are trying to make a difference.

The truth is that businesses will constantly have to go where their customers are congregating, and right now, consumers spend their days and nights frequenting social media sites. People are using social media channels to complain, praise companies and open up conversations about currently relevant issues. For consumers, this is a wonderful thing. It puts the control into the hands of the consumer and forces the business world to do the right thing. In today's online world of instant knowledge on any business or product, there is nowhere for companies to hide. And if you do hide behind your computers and automated phone robots, before long everyone will know about it and no one will trust you.

Here is the trick to using social media as a channel for you to improve customer service and make more sales. You must be fully engaged or not engaged at all. You have to fully commit as a business before taking this method on. Consistency is the key to your success when using social media, so if you're not willing or ready to invest the necessary amount of time and effort, do not get involved with it until you are willing and ready.

Why? Because there is nothing worse than seeing a company that has social media properties that never use them. I've seen Facebook business pages, for example, where potential customers have posted comments and the company has failed to reply or join in on the conversation. This 'sin of omission,' if you will, has the potential of killing your business one person at a time.

On the bright side, companies that use social media as a service tool are killing it! They are acquiring more customers, keeping more customers, and best of all making more profit - all because they are consciously engaged with their target.

There are so many ways that you as a company can use social media to help improve your business. You need to decide what are the most beneficial social media strategies for you and your business. We could write a whole book just on this topic. For now we want to give you one strategy to get started in the social media world.

We suggest you start with Twitter. Why? Because it is the fastest and easiest method to getting started. If you already have a Twitter account for your business then great, you're already on the right path. Here are five steps to using Twitter as a customer service channel.

What's your score? - www.TrustFactorBook.com/score

Step 1 – Set up a Twitter account at http://twitter.com/

Create a username that is unique to your business and tells people who you are. Make it 'catchy' or entertaining if appropriate. Don't use your name as the username unless your name is your brand.

Step 2 – Optimize your new Twitter account. Upload your logo and change the background of your profile to match your branding. Also, fill out all the personal and account information.

Step 3 – Download Tweetdeck at Tweetdeck.com then set up your Twitter account(s) within Tweetdeck. Yes, there are many other applications for Twitter, but this is the one we suggest to use. Another highly productive application available is Seesmic.com.

Step 4 – Next, add a column in Tweetdeck, (specifically a search option) with your company name and any keywords you would like to monitor on Twitter. That way, whenever the keyword you enter is mentioned on any of the millions of Twitter profiles, then the tweets (post or status updates on Twitter) will show up in that specific column.

Step 5 – Monitor, reply, and join the conversation. If people are talking about your products or complaining in any way, you can WOW them by helping them out with any issues they may have, hence improving your customer service. This also allows you to build relationships by being part of the conversation. This is what social media is all about.

The above five-step method is just a starting point when using Twitter. The key is to get started and stay consistent.

Alright. Let's recap the five important methods of transparency:

1 – Toll Free Phone Number
2 – Email (Ticket System)
3 – Live Chat

4 – Physical Address
5 – Social Media

Now ask yourself, what is your current level of transparency?

Is your business missing any of the essential methods discussed in this chapter? If so, then you need to seriously evaluate where your business is going. If you are just starting your business, then <u>now</u> is the time to determine how you are going to apply these strategies.

You must improve your customers' experience, and the only way to accomplish this is to consistently be engaged with them. The bottom line is that a good customer experience is going to help grow your business. In fact, there are books full of stories and examples of why amazing customer service pays off. The important thing to remember is to just do it! You already know why it's essential. Now you have a few proven methods to make it happen.

A perfect example of outstanding customer service that you should try to emulate is Zappos.com. With their free shipping BOTH ways on shoes and clothing, their 365-day return policy and 24/7 friendly customer service, it is no wonder they are killing the competition.

In July 2009, the company announced it would be acquired by Amazon.com in an all-stock deal worth about $1.2 billion, according to Wikipedia.com. Some speculate that the entire reason for the purchase was due to the fact that Amazon.com wanted to integrate the Zappos.com customer service culture and processes.

If you want to model an online company, Zappos.com is it. Here is one story that we thought was worth sharing.

According to an article by Meg Marco at Consumerist.com,

"Zaz Lamarr meant to return some shoes to Zappos, but her mom passed away and, naturally, she just didn't have time. Zappos arranged to have UPS come pick up the shoes—and then sent her flowers:

"When I came home this last time, I had an email from Zappos asking about the shoes, since they hadn't received them. I was just back and not ready to deal with that, so I replied that my mom had died but that I'd send the shoes as soon as I could. They emailed back that they had arranged with UPS to pick up the shoes, so I wouldn't have to take the time to do it myself. I was so touched. That's going against corporate policy.

Yesterday, when I came home from town, a florist delivery man was just leaving. It was a beautiful arrangement in a basket with white lilies and roses and carnations. Big and lush and fragrant. I opened the card, and it was from Zappos. I burst into tears. I'm a sucker for kindness, and if that isn't one of the nicest things I've ever had happen to me, I don't know what is."

This story has been shared over and over again. Think of all the good will Zappos received from this simple act of kindness. $30 for flowers could have got them hundreds of new loyal fans and customers. Pretty good return on their investment.

We aren't saying that you have to send flowers to all of your customers, but what we are saying is that the time is now for you to be more transparent, more thoughtful, and more engaged so that every customer and potential customer receives an incredible, memorable experience.

Chapter 4

Who Are You - Really?

Garrett and I are both huge fans of the TV show The Office. We both think that it's one of the funniest shows ever made.

In one of the episodes, Michael Scott (the office manager) is trying to get his staff to sign up for a pyramid scheme, oblivious to what he's actually doing of course. Toby (one of his employees) asks him, "Didn't you lose a lot of money on that other investment? The email?" To which Michael replies, "You know what Toby? When the son of the deposed king of Nigeria emails you directly, asking for help, you help! His father ran the freaking country! Okay?"

Good times...

Unfortunately, as crazy as it sounds, in the real-world thousands of people still fall for Nigerian scam emails and others like it every day.

In fact, according to an article in The Globe and Mail, actual Nigerian scammers claim that they get one to two genuine replies for every thousand emails they send. So, by doing some simple math, that means that if a scammer sent out just one million emails, he would get 2,000 hot leads, potentially stealing thousands, even millions of dollars from trusting, hard-working people just like you and me.

http://www.theglobeandmail.com/news/technology/article921349.ece

So how do Nigerian Scammers affect your business?

Well, thanks to the countless Nigerian scam emails that millions of Americans receive every day, in addition to a seemingly endless supply of news stories about credit card theft and identity theft, it's no surprise that online shoppers are continually becoming more concerned about the companies with which they do business. They want to know that the website they are buying from is actually a real business that they can trust.

Remember the Consumer Reports 'WebWatch' survey in Chapter 3 that stated that 81% of the people polled said that having access to a website's email address, street address and phone number was 'very important' to them?

Well, website owners who provide this contact information for their customers are taking a big step in the right direction. However, there is still a significant problem.

Nigerian scammers can add an email address, street address and phone number to their websites just as easy as you can.

Isn't that comforting?

Going back to Trust Factor #2 - The Art of Transparency - The reason any website, good or bad, adds business contact information is because it makes potential customers feel better about doing business with them. Realistically, very few if any customers actually ever attempt to contact the company before they do business with them. Yet by simply displaying the information, it creates a sense of company stability and trust.

So, the question arises, "How can you as a business owner effectively display your company contact information in a way that sets you apart as a trustworthy, reliable organization that people are more likely to do business with?"

The only way you can do this is through 3rd party business verification.

3rd party verification is the fastest, most effective way for people to trust you. It instantly shows your visitors that a trustworthy and reliable company, not associated with your business is vouching for you.

When you sign up for verification services from a well-respected 3rd party, they put your company through a thorough verification process to determine whether or not you are the person and company that you say you are.

Once the verification process is complete, the 3rd party verification company awards you a seal (a small image) that you can display on the front page and on the check out pages of your website. The seal links to a certificate that displays information related to your company so that visitors and potential customers can learn about you and the verification process that you successfully completed. It proves that your contact information has been verified and that you as a business owner really are who you say you are.

Do you remember Mary from Chapter Three?

Let's say that Mary got to your swimming suit website and felt somewhat comfortable because she felt like she could contact you if she needed. But deep inside she wasn't quite sure because she thought to herself, "Anybody can put an address or phone number on a website," which is a valid point.

Then to her delight she sees an image that says your company has recently been "VERIFIED" by a reliable 3rd party. She clicks on the button and is shown a certificate with detailed information about the company she is buying from, as well as the company that verified the information. Mary is now ready to buy. She feels comfortable about her decision to do business with you.

The key here is that you and your company must be verified by a reliable 3rd party. You can't just make a seal (image) that says you're verified, or that your friend verified your company. The reason why this won't work effectively is because most people visiting your website can tell the difference between real and fake verification.

Plus, people do a lot more research before they buy these days. So even if you do trick them with a simple image, what happens when they want to know who verified you? Then what?

When it comes to business verification, there are two main companies in the market.

The first company is the **Better Business Bureau**. The BBB states that its purpose is to collect information on business reliability, alert the public to frauds against consumers and businesses, provide information on ethical business practices, and act as a mutually trusted intermediary between consumers and businesses to resolve disputes.

Ultimately, the BBB has two advantages and two disadvantages. The two advantages are:

1) Branding - The BBB has been around for 100 years, and its brand is well established and credible. Once you become a paying member of the BBB (pricing typically runs $500/yr or more depending on the size of your business), you can display the BBB seal on your website.

2) Dispute Resolution Services - If your customers ever file a complaint, the BBB will act as a neutral party and help you resolve it.

The two disadvantages of the BBB, however, are significant - especially for online businesses. Unfortunately, most business owners don't realize the significance of these two issues it until it's too late.

1) The BBB gives you a letter grade based on a list of several criteria. Regrettably, some of their grading criteria is out of a business owner's control, like the type of business and age of the business. These factors, as well as the number of complaints received can give you a lower grade, creating doubt in the customer's mind.

2) The BBB publicly displays the number of complaints that your company receives. Even after you resolve the issue, they still show up on your BBB certificate for all new potential customers to see.

Bottom line, if you're a dependable, well-established company with a great customer service track record, the BBB can be a viable option and a great asset to your business. For more information, go to www.bbb.org and do a search for your zip code to find the BBB chapter for your location.

The second company that offers 3rd party verification is **Business Verified** by Trust Guard. While Business Verified hasn't been around nearly as long as the BBB, it offers similar services with a few important key differences.

1) Trust Guard caters specifically to online businesses. Unlike the BBB, which was built primarily to service brick and mortar companies, Business Verified is specifically designed to provide online companies with instant additional verification by providing customizable trust seals (the seals have both your name and the Trust Guard brand name on them) that add extra authenticity to the verification process. In addition, the Business Verified certificate shows the customers exactly what information has been verified and explains the verification process for additional peace of mind.

2) There is no grade level or company rating. Rather than creating the possibility of raising potential concerns before the customer ever decides to buy, Business Verified works on the "One-Strike-You're-Out" principle. In other words, companies that receive a complaint and simply don't respond or don't make a reasonable attempt to resolve it, can have their account temporarily suspended or canceled. While this may seem a bit harsh, it is a highly-effective way to sort the good apples from the bad.

3) Private Dispute Resolution Services. Business Verified services include private dispute resolution. Just like the BBB,

Business Verified acts as a neutral 3rd party. But unlike the BBB, once the issue is resolved the complaint does not show up on the company's certificate. Instead, the "One-Strike-You're-Out" policy ensures that businesses always take their customer complaints seriously. This eliminates the need to display resolved issues because every company actively displaying the Business Verified seals are in good standing.

4) Pricing. The price for Business Verified is considerably less expensive than the BBB. And unlike the BBB, the price doesn't increase over time as the size of your company increases.

Business Verified by Trust Guard may not have been around for 100 years, but they're definitely a solid choice when it comes to choosing a business verification company. Visit http://www.trustguard.com/Business-Seals-s/76.htm to learn about the Business Verified seal and service.

Although this may feel like a waste of time, the simple act of adding business verification services could significantly increase your sales. In fact, we have seen numerous businesses that, just by simply placing a 3rd party business verification seal on their website, have received a significant increase in sales.

Here is a case study where just one simple Business Verified seal quickly increased opt-ins (leads) by 16.51%.

A Place For Mom Case Study

When you're running a split test, the larger the sample size, the more accurate the results. It also happens that additional traffic gives you the ability to test more variables. This was the case with a split test for aplaceformom.com.

Aplaceformom.com is one of the largest online lead generation websites for retirement homes across the country. They receive about 250,000 visitors a month. Because of their high traffic volume, they were able to do something unique – they split tested 32 verification seal combinations all at the same time to find the highest converting seal for their particular needs.

The split test included different colors, sizes, and styles – which were then rotated in a single position on their site, directly underneath their application form. In addition to the 32 verification seals, they also rotated a blank option, where no seals showed up. After the first round of testing, they narrowed the test down to the top eight performing seals (nine including the blank option).

In the second round, a clear winner began to emerge to the point where it beat all other options. Most visible in the results was how the winner beat the blank 'no seal' option by a whopping 16.51% with a 98% confidence interval. The winner was the small blue Business Verified seal by Trust Guard. By adding this seal to the bottom of their application, they now receive several thousand more applications per month than they had before they started using verification seals.

Just let that sink in for a minute.

Imagine the impact that a 16.51% instant increase in leads would have on your existing business.

Let's do some math. Suppose you are currently getting 1025 leads a day on average and you're pretty happy with that number. By adding verification seals to your website, you bump up your leads by 16.51% or an extra 170 leads per day. That's an extra 5100 leads per month and all you did was give your visitors what they want - to know they can TRUST you with their personal information.

So, should you stop what you're doing right now and go buy the small blue Business Verified seal for your site? Not necessarily. It's important to remember that each website is unique and has different demographics, so what works on one site may not work on another. Who knows? Maybe a red color will work better for your market and your website. You just don't know until you test.

The bottom line is that you need to be aware that people are not as trusting as they used to be. You need to give them a way to feel comfortable before they will be willing to give you their information and part with their money. Skip this strategy at your own risk!

Chapter 5

Private Parts

Growing up, we learn very quickly not to talk to strangers, share secrets and especially to never give someone our personal information like our names or where we live or what our phone number is if we don't know and trust them. We have been hardwired into having a skeptical and cautious nature. There is nothing wrong with this, especially in today's world. With sexual predators, identity thieves, scam artists and plain old bad people, it's no wonder we have to be extremely careful.

These days social networking sites and search engines love to watch our every move. People are becoming more worried about how their private information is being shared. If they are asked to give their personal information on a website, they want to know exactly how the online company intends on sharing their information.

Columbia University recently reported a study of theirs in the Huffington Post:

"The research, which tracked the Facebook use of 65 students ages 18 to 25, found that 100 percent of the participants were sharing personal information online in ways they had not intended.

Though 95 percent of the participants were initially confident their online privacy settings "matched their attitude toward privacy," all 65 wound up reporting sharing violations -- meaning personal data they wished to hide was public or information they wished to share was hidden.

Eighty-four percent of the participants discovered their privacy settings had mistakenly concealed details they had meant to disclose, whereas more than ninety-three percent realized they were revealing information they had wanted to cover up.

The participants described online privacy policies as a key factor in defending against threats to their social, economic and physical well-being. Concern over physical safety was the most commonly cited explanation for hiding personal information on Facebook. Yet when asked about the most important reason for online privacy, 49 percent cited protecting their reputation, 38 percent said it was necessary to safeguard against identity theft and other economic risks and just 12 percent pointed to threats to their security." - http://www.huffingtonpost.com/2011/04/13/online-privacy-settings-study_n_848771.html

Remember the story of Mary in Chapter Three? She was extra careful about who she would do business with online.

Online businesses have to understand the importance of making visitors feel welcome and safe. It's absolutely essential to running a successful online business.

You must put yourself in the shoes of your visitor or prospect. Do *you* like to give out your personal information like your email address, physical address, phone number and credit card? Well, neither do your customers.

Think of it this way. Most people don't even like giving their credit card number and personal information to their own family members. And yet you - someone that they have never met is asking for it. There is a huge TRUST issue going on subconsciously or even consciously in the visitor's head. He or she may be very interested in your product or service, but there is always a mental barrier that must come down in order to close the deal. This is what 'The TRUST Factor' is all about: breaking the mental fear barrier.

Many people will not make an online purchase unless they know that their personal and private information are going to be kept safe. They need to know that you as the company will not share, sell or lose that private information. They must TRUST you before they are going to take any type of action, such as filling out a form, giving you their email, and most of all giving you their credit card.

There was a survey done by Unisys Security Index. It said that people are more concerned about their credit card being stolen than terrorism, computer viruses, and their own personal safety. Can you believe that? (In the next chapter we are going to go into more detail of how to keep people's information safe and secure. It's a chapter you cannot afford to miss.)

This chapter is focused around two very important TRUST factors that are critical to your success. If customers expect privacy and have privacy concerns (which they all do) then you must implement the following two policies into your website:

- Professional Privacy Policy
- Terms of Service Agreement

The following list mentions some of the cases where a website **Privacy Policy** is required:

- If you are collecting personal information from any California residents, *even if you don't live in California*, then California state law requires you to post a privacy policy. This law basically requires every ecommerce website to have a privacy policy, since at some point they are all likely to do business with a California resident.
- If you process credit card transactions online, your credit card processor may require you to post a privacy policy as a part of your merchant agreement.
- If you display Google AdSense advertising on your website, Google requires you to "post and abide by a transparent privacy policy that users see" as a part of your publishers agreement.
- If your website is directed towards children or collects personal data from children under the age of 13, federal

law requires a privacy policy that follows strict guidelines.

- If your website is a financial institution (and this includes retail stores that extend credit to their customers), federal law requires you to post a privacy policy.

- If you are a health care professional or plan provider, such as a doctor or pharmacy, federal law requires you to post a privacy policy.

Resources:
Gwinnett Business Journal – "Policing Your Privacy Policy"
Google AdSense privacy policy requirements
Children's Online Privacy Protection Act of 1998
Gramm-Leach-Billey Financial Modernization Act of 1999
Health Insurance Portability and Accountability Act of 1996 (HIPAA)
* List above provided by Lindsey Marshall of Redclay Interactive

When it comes to a **Terms of Service Agreement** (also known as TOS, Term of Use, Terms and Conditions, etc.) you must keep in mind that you have a lawful affiliation with everyone who visits your website, whether they buy anything or even identify themselves. It's to your benefit and advantage to set the terms of that relationship with a user terms and conditions agreement. Essentially, you are setting the terms by which the visitor/member/customer can use your website.

Show your customers that you take their privacy seriously by properly generating these two policies. If you already have these policies on your website, then you may want to review them and make sure that they meet all the current regulations and mandates.

Most of what we see out there are website owners who have gone to a big name website and copied their privacy and terms-of-service policies. It is easy to tell when people do this. Sure, they change a couple of words and replace the domain and company name with their own, but in most cases the policies don't reflect their own values or even their own industry! This is just crazy.

First of all, your policies are most likely unique to you. For example, you may process or store your customers' information in a certain way, or you might use their information to contact them or promote future products through an opt-in process. You might even pass on certain information to a 3rd party. Whatever the case, your company is held accountable to what you present on any policy you have on your website, so it is imperative that your policies accurately reflect your company's processes and procedures.

Secondly, you have no right to copy what someone else has created without their permission. Are your existing policies simply copied from another website? If so, whether you realize it or not, you're committing copyright infringement and may be putting yourself and your company at risk of a possible law suit.

Instead of you wasting time and effort trying to figure out the particular details of what exactly has to be in a privacy policy and terms of service agreement, here are two ways that you can create your own:

- Fork out money and get a lawyer to create one for you. (Pricing will vary based on the city you live in and the firm you decide to go with.)
- Search your favorite search engine for articles on how to create these policies and everything that must be included. (This can take hours and even days of research.)

Okay, we know that sounds like either a lot of work or a lot of money. Fortunately, there is a third option. We have done all the legwork already and have created a privacy policy generator and terms of service generator that are by far the best out there. If you're reading this book and have already used our services, you know how easy they are to create with our software.

What's your score? - www.TrustFactorBook.com/score

Here is where you can go to get a professional privacy policy and terms of service agreement for your website:

- ProfessionalPrivacyPolicy.com
- TermsofServiceGenerator.com

Both services provide innovative point-and-click type questions that walk you through the creation process, helping you to develop your own custom, easy-to-read policies. Yes, these are paid services, but the small one-time investment is well worth it – especially considering the alternatives. The best part is that you can literally have both policies on your website within 30 minutes. (Note: we always recommend having any policy you create reviewed by a legal representative.)

Once you have created your policies, you must place them somewhere on your website that can be easily accessed by your potential and current customers. In most cases, that means that a link to your privacy policy needs to be somewhere on your front page. We suggest you put links to each policy in the footer of every page on your website, but at a minimum on your home page. Also, the links need to be specific. For example, your privacy policy anchor text needs to have the word "Privacy" in it. The same goes for your Terms of Service link text. This fulfills legal requirements. It also gives your visitors an easy way to find your policies.

Do people actually read the policies? Well, you might be surprised. It's likely that many of your visitors won't – at least the entire policy. But just having it there is often enough to give them what they do need; those warm and fuzzy feelings that reassure them that you are going to keep their private information safe. If they can see that you have the necessary policies, even if they don't read them all, most online consumers will be satisfied enough to buy from you.

Having these policies also protects you as a business. For example, having a proper Terms of Service agreement helps you to outline your website's copyright and trademark policies in order to curb infringement and unauthorized use. Also, if there ever was a problem, or heaven forbid, a lawsuit, these policies can become a very big tool in protecting your rights. This is especially true if you've outlined the relationship, roles, and responsibilities that both you and your customers have to each other.

Although this chapter can be somewhat mind numbing when talking about legal matters, we'd like to lighten the mood by giving you the financial benefits of implementing these important methods of transparency and how they relate to the Trust Factor.

If you added a privacy policy and TOS agreement to your website and it increased your sales by even two percent, would it be worth it? Let's go even further and say that you went to a reliable 3rd party and went through the necessary steps to get verified. Accordingly, you would become 'Privacy Verified' and the 3rd party would confirm to your customers that your site is trustworthy. Then, that verification company would give you a privacy seal image that you could copy and paste onto your website for all your visitors to see. Do you think that would improve the perception of your website or company in the visitor's eyes or mind? What if just placing that privacy seal on your website increased your sales by five percent? Would that help your business?

Let's put this into numbers. Say you have a product that is a $497 one-time payment. You are currently getting about 100 sales a month. Then you add a privacy policy, TOS agreement and privacy seal to your website and you get a five percent increase in sales. That amounts to an extra 60 sales a year with an additional $29,820 in revenue. Now that sounds pretty good, right? Of course your results will vary, but we have seen companies get as high as a sixty percent increase in sales just by displaying seals on their site that demonstrate to their visitors that they are trustworthy. That is powerful!

So you're probably wondering where you can get a 3rd party

verified privacy seal for your website. There are two reputable privacy verification companies we recommend that offer a privacy seal in addition to their privacy verification services - Truste and Trust Guard. We'll let you decide which company best fits your needs. Both companies provide great services.

Chapter 6

Security is King

Remember the good old days when all you needed was an SSL certificate to secure your transactions online? Back in the late 90's, during the first few years of our online clothing business, we kept all our customer's information in online file folders - even their credit cards. In those days, if any data was encrypted, we would be very surprised. Pretty sure it wasn't secure.

The crazy thing is that most online businesses back then used to do business that way; without security. It wasn't that we didn't want to keep our customer's information safe. It was just that we assumed it was safe and we didn't know any better at the time. The shopping cart software we used automatically created the files with private data and put them on our server, so I guess you could blame the lack of security on them if you wanted to. But the truth is, it just never crossed our minds that the information could be at risk back then. Fortunately for us, nothing ever happened.

Fast forward to the present day when security has quickly become a top priority online. These days, damaging threats like viruses, adware, spyware, hacker attacks and even identity theft and fraud are a common occurrence.

Case in point: Over the past decade we've seen some serious security breaches in the news. Below are a few of the major security hacks that might surprise you:

Credit And Debit Card Breach May Affect Over 100 Million
January 21, 2009
The Washington Post has reported that Heartland Payment Systems, a payment processor that services "more than 250,000

businesses," has had more than 100 million transactions compromised via malicious software that was installed on its network...

Citi Credit Card Security Breach Discovered
June 9, 2011
NEW YORK (CNNMoney) -- Citigroup says it has discovered a security breach in which a hacker accessed personal information from hundreds of thousands of accounts. Citigroup said the breach occurred last month and affected about 200,000 customers...

T.J. Maxx Theft Believed Largest Hack Ever
March 30, 2007
BOSTON — A hacker or hackers stole data from at least 45.7 million credit and debit cards of shoppers at off-price retailers including T.J. Maxx and Marshalls in a case believed to be the largest such breach of consumer information. For the first time since disclosing the theft more than two months ago, the parent company of nearly 2,500 discount stores put a number on how much card data was compromised — and it's a number TJX Cos. acknowledges could go still higher...

Network Solutions Hack Compromises 573,000 Credit, Debit Accounts
July 24, 2009
Hackers have broken into Web servers owned by domain registrar and hosting provider Network Solutions, planting rogue code that resulted in the compromise of more than 573,000 debit and credit card accounts over the past three months.

Network Solutions discovered in early June that attackers had hacked into Web servers the company uses to provide ecommerce services to at least 4,343 customers, mostly mom-and-pop online stores. The malicious code left behind by the attackers allowed them to intercept personal and financial information for customers who purchased from those stores, Network Solutions spokeswoman Susan Wade said...

These are just a tiny drop in the bucket compared to the thousands of security breaches that have taken place since 2000.

So, here's the million dollar question: Are internet sites safer now than they were ten years ago? In some ways yes, thanks to better shopping cart software and 3rd party checkout services like Paypal. But unfortunately, a significant number of ecommerce websites are still putting their customers and themselves at significant risk, and many of them don't even know it.

How significant is this security problem? Well, according to Clone Systems, a leading Security Scanning company online, approximately 86% of all ecommerce websites have at least one or more medium, high, or severe vulnerabilities that could put their customers and their website at risk of being compromised by hackers.

They know this because out of all of the thousands of websites that they scan on a regular basis, 86% of them failed their initial vulnerability scan.

Just to put that into perspective, approximately 9 out of every 10 transactions that you make online, where you think that your information is safe, are actually at risk.

Pretty scary isn't it?

Here's why most sites are at risk:

Just like our online clothing store back in the day, most

ecommerce websites have an SSL certificate. Understandably, the store owner assumes that since they have an active SSL certificate, their customer's transactions will be processed safely and reach their destination safely. This is all true.

There's only one problem.

Once the customer's information reaches its destination, it is stored on a server for future reference. This information can include the customer's name, email, address, phone number, and credit card information. And sometimes it even includes social security numbers and personal financial information.

Although most people don't realize it, this information often sits on a server for months, or even years. This is when customer information is most vulnerable. It's customer databases like these that hackers are anxiously looking for and trying to access. SSL only encrypts the initial transaction. However, once the information gets to its final destination, it's vulnerable from that point on. But don't take my word for it, just ask TJ Maxx.

So, what are your options as a website owner?

Well, you basically have three options available to you.

Option 1 – SSL only. This is actually still an option, but it's quickly disappearing as PCI SSC standards continue to tighten (We explain this in option 3 below).

Option 2 – Use a 3rd party payment processor (ie. PayPal, Clickbank, 2Checkout). This is a great option if you're a small company and you are just starting out online for two reasons:

> First, it's easy to implement. All you do is copy and paste some code on your site and checkout buttons automatically appear on your website where people can buy. Once customers click on the buttons, they are redirected to the 3rd party payment processor where they can checkout with full security measures in place.

Second, there are no monthly fees. All your fees come out of the transaction which means you'll pay more per transaction, but you'll save money initially.

The downside of a 3rd party payment processor is that you may lose some credibility – especially if this is your only payment method. However, the opposite can actually be true as well. You can actually increase your credibility if you combine Paypal with traditional credit card options (by getting a merchant account). Just as an interesting side note, our PayPal transactions typically account for about 25-30% of all our sales.

Option 3 – Use SSL and a PCI Security Scanning service together with a merchant account for maximum security. This is the recommended option for all ecommerce companies online, and it's primarily due to an organization called the PCI SSC. If you've never heard of the PCI SSC, this is definitely something that you need to know about.

The PCI SSC stands for the Payment Card Industry Security Standards Council. This is a council created by the Payment Card Industry, which consists of VISA, MasterCard, American Express, Discover and others for the purpose of creating standardized security measures in order to improve safety and security online.

Over the past few years, the PCI SSC has put various security standards in place that ecommerce websites, and any other companies that do any type of credit card transactions have to meet in order to receive a merchant account.

They've actually created a very detailed, comprehensive 12-part PCI Compliant checklist that they expect all companies who process any type of credit card transactions to follow. Fortunately, they only require it from companies that do over a million transactions per year. [By the way, if you're a glutton for punishment, go to their website and try reading their documentation.]

What's your score? - www.TrustFactorBook.com/score

The rest of us have a much more simplified process for becoming PCI Compliant. We are only required to complete a quarterly PCI Security Scan and fill out an annual PCI Self-Assessment Questionnaire (SAQ).

The PCI Security Scan examines and inspects your website for tens of thousands of known vulnerabilities to find out if you have any security issues that hackers could use to get unauthorized access to your server.

Once the scan is complete, it creates two reports. The first report is a detailed list of all the vulnerabilities that were found during the scan, along with the severity of the vulnerabilities and instructions on how they can be resolved. If your website failed the scan with one or more medium, high, or severe vulnerabilities, then you simply forward the detailed report to your hosting company or server administrator to fix, and then you run another scan when the issues are resolved. Once you've successfully passed the scan, you send a copy of the second report, which is called an Executive Report, to your merchant provider as proof that you successfully passed the scan.

When you submit a copy of your PCI Executive Report, your merchant provider will also ask you for a copy of your annual PCI Self-Assessment Questionnaire (SAQ). (The SAQ form is usually provided along with the scanning service.) Simply fill out the SAQ form, and submit it along with your PCI Scan Executive Report to become PCI Compliant.

Being PCI Compliant is actually a really good thing because it protects you from serious penalties and fines that the PCI SSC can impose on you if you're not compliant. But even more important than that, once you've successfully become compliant, and passed your PCI scan, you can immediately start leveraging that information to help build customer trust by displaying trust seals on your website. This leverage can be incredibly powerful, and can set you apart from your competitors while boosting your sales!

When it comes time to choose an online PCI Security Scanning company, there are several to choose from. But only a handful of them offer security seals (images) that you can add to your website to show your customers that your website is safe. Three of the main companies that include security trust seals are McAfee Secure, HackerProof, and Security Scanned by Trust Guard.

McAfee Secure is the largest PCI scanning company online. Unfortunately, they're also one of the most expensive, with daily scanning starting at around $2,000 a year and then increasing based on traffic. HackerProof is also in the $2,000 annual price range.

Alternatively, Security Scanned by Trust Guard is significantly less expensive, starting at about a quarter of the cost while offering more value and options than the competition.

Once you have your security in place, make sure that you share your efforts with your online visitors. It's time now to show your customers that your website is safe. There are two ways to do this. You can either place big text on your website that tells visitors that your site is safe, or you use a 3rd party seal that includes a certificate that tells them that your site is safe.

Most of the companies that we mentioned above offer a security seal to place on your website. You would be doing yourself and your visitors a big disservice if you failed to display a seal on your website. Why? Because this is where the Trust Factor comes into play. By showing your customers that your website is safe and secure, they feel more comfortable and confident in buying from your website. And because they trust you, your conversion rate will increase.

We suggest that you place your 3rd party Security Scanned seal on your home page, product pages, and especially your checkout pages where the customer is entering their private information.

Unlike any other PCI scanning company online, Security

Scanned by Trust Guard is the only service that offers a backup feature when a PCI scan fails. If a scan fails with McAfee Secure or HackerProof, the trust seal disappears until the issue is resolved, leaving your website without any security seal. But with Security Scanned, the seal simply changes to a Security Verified status, enabling you to continue displaying a security verification seal in place of a security seal until any issues are resolved.

One of the important things to remember about PCI Security Scanning is that all scans are done by a PCI Approved Scanning Vendor (ASV). This means that whichever company you choose, they all have to scan your website using the same security standards, otherwise they can't be PCI approved.

Sometimes people wonder why PCI scanning companies offer daily scanning if only quarterly scanning is required to be PCI compliant. Well, the main reason that companies offer daily scanning is because daily scanning offers better overall protection. There are typically over 100 new vulnerabilities found every week, and if you only scan quarterly, that means that your website could be vulnerable to 1,200 or more new vulnerabilities before your next scan. So, by scanning daily, you ensure that your server is protected as quickly as possible. The other reason that daily scans are preferred is because customers feel more comfortable knowing that the websites they are visiting are scanned every day.

Just think about it. Would you rather buy from a website that scans their system against hackers every 3 months or every day? Daily, right? So would your customers.

At the end of the day, security is king - especially for ecommerce sites. The more you can do to make your customers feel safe and secure, the more they are going to trust you and your website and the more likely they are to buy from you.

On the other hand, not having both an SSL certificate and PCI scanning in place is like playing Russian roulette with your business. There are so many ways that a hacker can infiltrate your server, that to stay in business online business owners have to take a proactive approach. Otherwise it's just a matter of time before they get access and you suddenly find yourself informing your customers why their information was stolen and how you didn't take the proper measures to protect it.

You'll also have to explain to the PCI SSC what happened and will most likely end up being fined and/or having your merchant account taken away. It's just not worth the risk to not scan your site for vulnerabilities, especially when you can use security to your advantage by displaying seals that will build trust and help you make even more sales.

Security is definitely one expense that pays for itself – especially online.

Here is a quick security self-assessment:

Do you and your employees have active and updated anti-virus software installed on your computer(s)?

Where are you hosting your website? Is your server dedicated or shared?

Does your website have an up-to-date SSL certificate? Is all confidential data encrypted?

Has your website ever been hacked?

Do you share sensitive information within the company? If so, is every participating member of the staff aware of it, and do they have their own unique password?

Is your website PCI Scanned at least quarterly?

If you answered "NO" to any of the previous questions, you may have some work to do. Don't take your website's security for granted. Doing so might just put you out of business.

Chapter 7

We 'Guarantee' You'll
Love This Chapter

Have you ever made a promise that you didn't keep?

How did it make you feel? Pretty lousy right? You probably got
that sinking feeling in the pit of your stomach and had a sudden
urge to go hide in a dark cave for a while.

But what about the other side of the coin?

Hasn't there been a time in your life when you made a promise
and then kept it? You felt great! You had the full satisfaction
and peace of mind in knowing that you are a person of your
word and that your moral compass points true north.

But what do keeping promises have to do with running a
successful business? Well, everything.

Whenever you make a promise to anyone, even if it is a
customer, you enter into a morally binding agreement with that
person. It doesn't matter how big or small the promise might be.
You create an obligation to keep it.

But when it comes to business, there is a very special, unique
promise you can make that stands out above all other promises.
In fact, this one promise is so important that it can single-
handedly make or break your online success. Without it, you
lose your competitive edge and blend in with the crowd. But
with it, you stand out from everyone else, and have the
opportunity to significantly boost your conversion rate.

It's the GUARANTEE.

What's your score? - www.TrustFactorBook.com/score

And we're not just talking about any guarantee. We are talking about a KILLER guarantee!

Speaking of guarantees, let's have a bit of fun. See if you remember the movie that the following dialogue about guarantees comes from:

> "Tommy: Let's think about this for a sec, Ted. Why would somebody put a guarantee on a box? Hmmm, very interesting.
>
> Ted Nelson (customer): Go on, I'm listening.
>
> Tommy: Here's the way I see it, Ted. Guy puts a fancy guarantee on a box 'cause he wants you to feel all warm and toasty inside.
>
> Ted Nelson (customer): Yeah, makes a man feel good.
>
> Tommy: 'Course it does. Why shouldn't it? Ya figure you put that little box under your pillow at night, the Guarantee Fairy might come by and leave a quarter, am I right, Ted?
> [chuckles until he sees that Ted is not laughing]
>
> Ted Nelson (customer): [impatiently] What's your point?
>
> Tommy: The point is, how do you know the fairy isn't a crazy glue sniffer? "Building model airplanes" says the little fairy; well, we're not buying it. He sneaks into your house once, that's all it takes. The next thing you know, there's money missing off the dresser, and your daughter's knocked up. I seen it a hundred times.
>
> Ted Nelson (customer): But why do they put a guarantee on the box?
>
> Tommy: Because they know all they sold ya was a guaranteed piece of s***. That's all it is, isn't it? Hey, if

you want me to take a dump in a box and mark it guaranteed, I will. I got spare time. But for now, for your customer's sake, for your daughter's sake, ya might wanna think about buying a quality product from me.

Ted Nelson (customer): [pause] Okay, I'll buy from you.

Tommy: Well, that's... What?"

The quote above is from the brash, but very funny 1995 movie 'Tommy Boy'.

Although in the clip he's actually knocking guarantees, we share this quote with you to ingrain into your mind FIRST the importance of having a great or even outstanding product. No, your product or service doesn't have to be perfect. It simply has to do what you say it will do.

One reason why there is a trust issue between buyers and customers in the first place is because everyone at one point or another has bought a 'crappy' product (thanks Tommy). You know, something that looked great in the box or on the website then turned out to be completely different than what they thought they were buying.

In other words, it doesn't matter if you give the most mind-blowing guarantee in the world, if your product or service doesn't end up helping the customer or living up to their expectations, your company simply won't make it. You have to deliver quality. Consistent quality.

Now that we know the importance of a having a quality product or service, it is time to talk about the power of the guarantee. Also known as a:

- Promise
- Warranty
- Certification

- Pledge
- Assurance
- Endorsement

Call it what you may, in this chapter we refer to it as a guarantee. Most often, to close the deal you must offer a promise of a money-back guarantee. With a guarantee, you eliminate the buyer risk, therefore eliminating any lingering barriers standing in the way of the sale.

Just adding text on your website that says, "Guarantee" or "We Promise" is not going to cut it these days. Hopefully by this chapter you now realize (if you didn't already) that people are distrustful. Therefore, you need to construct the guarantee to be compelling, motivating and realistic.

If you are able to remove any presumed risk from your prospects' eyes, they will click the "Buy Now" button. You have to convince your buyer that not only is your product or service going to help them but that if it doesn't then you are willing to stand behind your product by giving them their money back (or some other guarantee that benefits the customer).

Here are three examples of a guarantee (good, better and best):

GOOD –

> Use my Blue Widget service for the next 30 days and increase your sales or we'll give you a full refund.

BETTER –

> Give our Blue Widget a try now, risk-free! If it doesn't improve your sales in the next 60 days, or if, for any reason, you're not completely satisfied with it, just let us know and we will give you a no-hassle full refund.

BEST –

> We're so confident that our Blue Widget service will increase your sales that we'll take all the risk. Go ahead and try our services completely RISK-FREE for <u>an entire year</u>. And if for any reason you're not absolutely thrilled, then we will give you DOUBLE YOUR MONEY BACK, no questions asked!

Keep in mind that these are just examples. Each industry and market has their own needs. This is something that you will need to test.

Here are some things to consider when creating your guarantee:

- **Keep it easy to understand** – no one wants to read a bunch of legal jargon to understand how your guarantee works, give them exactly what they need and keep the details, if there are any, in your Terms of Service agreement.

- **Don't mislead your prospect** – avoid trying to deceive your potential customers. They will see right through you, which will defeat the purpose of a guarantee.

- **Be authentic and truthful** – remember that your business rests on the moral shoulders of integrity and TRUST.

- **Plan ahead** – before you write your guarantee, make sure that you think of all the possibilities that could occur if someone asks for a refund. Ask yourself if you are willing to follow through with your guarantee no matter what. This will save you a lot of possible problems simply by deciding now.

Some of you are probably re-reading the 'Best' option above and thinking to yourselves, "Are these guys crazy? How can anyone offer a full year double your money back guarantee?" Although we may be crazy, we have been using this guarantee for years and it has worked extremely well. In fact, over the past four years that we have been offering this guarantee, we have only had one person ask for double their money back.

Why? Well, first of all, our services are outstanding. Secondly, we have found that no one wants to be 'that guy.' You know what we mean. No one wants to ask for double their money back when the product or service really did help them, or in many cases, they never actually used the product to its full potential. For this very reason, along with our 'One Year Double Your Money Back Guarantee' we offer a normal 60-day money back guarantee. We understand that our products and services don't always work for everyone and therefore we are always willing to give our customers 60 days to use our products, if they aren't happy or the product didn't fit what they need, then we never hesitate to give their money back.

As an interesting side note, there have been a few times over the years when clients have actually qualified for the double your money back guarantee for one reason or another. Surprisingly they always ask for a full refund instead of requesting that we double their money back.

In most cases, we believe you should give the refund when requested – even if it is not earned. It is not worth having an unhappy customer who will give you bad reviews, write on complaint boards or even worse, start a social media campaign against you. Also, give the refund as soon as you can. Don't wait. There are no correct timelines in giving a refund, but what we suggest is at least within 24-48 hours.

Here is what will happen if you give the customer the correct refund in a timely manner:

- You will make that person happy even if they weren't pleased with your product/service. In most cases, they will not talk poorly about you, which could otherwise cost you some sales and deflate your reputation.

- More than likely you will build a good relationship with this person that can grow into a lifelong relationship (if you do it correctly). In fact, an unsatisfied customer turned satisfied is often more loyal than those who were satisfied to begin with.

- If you listen to your customers and truly understand their needs, you can sell this person different products or services that may better fit their needs. Even if the product is from a competitor, if you help the customer, they will remember your kindness. The opposite is also true. Last weekend, while our friend Aaron was on vacation in the Seattle area, he and his family went to McDonalds for breakfast. It turns out they were ten minutes late. When he asked if the attendant knew of another restaurant close by that was still serving breakfast, after a pause, she responded that she didn't. He drove around the corner and lo-and-behold there was a Denny's. It wasn't a half a block from the McDonalds. All we're saying is tell them there is a Denny's a half a block away if there is one. Next time, they'll wake up earlier!

- You can learn from their concerns and use them to help improve your company's products and processes. Why not ask for their suggestions to improve it? You might be surprised how many unsatisfied customers are willing to help you make a better product! This will help you make future customers happy which will lead to more sales.

If a high percent of customers (over 1%) are asking for refunds, you need to look at your sales funnel and more importantly your end product. If you have good products or services, then it might be something as easy as getting a new delivery courier.

Keep in mind that there are some markets where refunds are

higher than others. You need to know your market and be willing to change if needed. We suggest you consult with legal counsel before offering a guarantee.

We know that giving a guarantee can make you feel a little vulnerable. You don't want to take the chance of losing money or dealing with the reality that customers may not like your product. It is time to get over this fear and face it dead on.

Seriously, why not try it out? What have you got to lose? In reality, offering a killer guarantee is a lot less scary that it sounds.

Your competitors will be shocked and intimidated when they see that you are offering a double your money back guarantee (or a better guarantee than what they offer). Anyone can give a 30-day money back guarantee, but a company that is truly confident offers a more confident guarantee and therefore receives more TRUST.

Always remember: a guarantee is only as good as the people who stand behind it, so be ready to stand up.

As with any type of offer, especially double your money back, you must always be very specific of the terms in the guarantee. You can make those terms known within your Terms of Service agreement. Here is an example of our terms for one of our products:

> "Rhino Support Platinum member services come with both a 60 day money back guarantee and a one (1) year double your money back guarantee. These two guarantees are explained below:
>
> 60 day money back guarantee - In order to qualify for the 60 day money back guarantee, if you are unsatisfied with our services for any reason, simply contact our support staff within the first 60 days of subscribing to any of the Platinum membership packages, and we will

gladly and quickly give you a full refund.

One (1) year double your money back guarantee - In order to qualify for the double your money back guarantee, you need to have actively used Rhino Support as a Platinum member for the first 12 months of service. If after one (1) full year, you are unsatisfied with our services for any reason, you can request either a full refund or double your money back, whichever you prefer, anytime within the 13th month of service, and we will honor your request accordingly. The double your money back guarantee is only valid during the 13th month of service."

- http://rhinosupport.com/terms.htm

As you can see, we are very specific in describing what each guarantee entails.

In our opinion, either you offer a guarantee that is outstanding or don't offer one at all. If you decide to go with the crowd and post a cookie-cutter 30 day money back guarantee instead of offering a killer guarantee, then you might as well not offer one. People are smarter than you might think and they can usually smell an unauthentic person/product/service out of the crowd. That doesn't mean that there aren't companies out there that pull the wool over some people's eyes. But in doing so, they remove the TRUST Factor and will not be building a long-lasting business.

The real question here is, do you stand by your product or not?

Here is text straight from the FTC website on general offers and claims for products and services:

"The Federal Trade Commission Act allows the FTC to act in the interest of all consumers to prevent deceptive and unfair acts or practices. In interpreting Section 5 of the Act, the Commission has determined that a representation, omission or practice is deceptive if it is likely to:

mislead consumers and affect consumers' behavior or decisions about the product or service...

...The FTC Act prohibits unfair or deceptive advertising in any medium. That is, advertising must tell the truth and not mislead consumers. A claim can be misleading if relevant information is left out or if the claim implies something that's not true...

... Disclaimers and disclosures must be clear and conspicuous. That is, consumers must be able to notice, read or hear, and understand the information...

... Refunds must be made to dissatisfied consumers - if you promised to make them."

Resource:
(http://business.ftc.gov/documents/bus28-advertising-and-marketing-internet-rules-road)

If you are a legitimate business, there is no reason for concern when reading the above statement. The FTC is just simply keeping it real and setting some guidelines for all those scam artists out there. You should spend a significant amount of time when crafting your guarantee, ensuring that you are willing to deliver on what you guarantee.

In closing this chapter, we want to impress upon you the importance of being able to back up your killer guarantee. Your killer guarantee has to be backed by amazing customer service, and your amazing customer service has to be backed by a great product. If these items are in place, then your company is bound for growth and greatness.

Have you ever heard stories of Nordstrom and their amazing customer service and policies? Here are a couple of stories that we found in an article called "Legends of Unbelievable Nordstrom Service" at toddand.com:

> "Legends of Nordstrom pampering are widespread. Nordstrom thrives on providing memorable experiences and creating customer folklore. Every register at Nordstrom stores has pen and paper for customers to share their stories. Every morning before each store opens, Nordstrom employees gather in the main lobby for the store manager to share some of the best stories from the previous day and reward the employees in those stories. And, in talking with many Nordstrom customers recently, it seems like every customer has their own legendary Nordstrom tale, or has at least heard one.
>
> Have you heard about the customer who tried to return pants that had clearly been worn for an extended amount of time, but was still refunded? Or the Nordstrom employee who made a house call to exchange a pair of shoes? How about the blouse that was returned and refunded when it was clearly from another store? And then there's the one about Nordstrom splitting two pairs of shoes in order to fit the man with different sized feet.
>
> One legendary story is the "tire chains" story. A man walked into Nordstrom and insisted that he purchased a used set of tire chains there. Without hesitation, the Nordstrom clerk refunded the person's money out of her own pocket – even though the receipt clearly indicated another store. Then, on her lunch hour, she took the receipt and tire chains to the store where they were from and got her money back.
>
> Another famed story is of the Portland man who needed an Armani tuxedo for his daughter's wedding. As a last-ditch effort to find an Armani tuxedo, he went to the local Nordstrom. His personal shopper took his measurements and asked for a little time to work on it.

What's your score? - www.TrustFactorBook.com/score

The customer left and the next day he received a phone call from Nordstrom saying they had found the tux and it would be ready the next day. The next day he drove to Nordstrom, tried on the tux and found it fit perfectly. Nordstrom had altered the tux for free. He asked his Nordstrom personal shopper how she did it. She just smiled and shrugged "magic." He pressed and the Nordstrom personal shopper explained that after he left the store she had immediately worked to solve the problem by utilizing her connections and finding the tux on the other side of the continent in New York. The New York distributor put the Armani tux on a truck bound for Chicago that day where the personal shopper had coordinated for a Chicago Nordstrom employee to meet the truck at a rest stop and retrieve the tux. Once in the Chicago Nordstrom store, the tux was over-nighted to Portland and altered to fit perfectly. The unbelievable service? Nordstrom doesn't even sell Armani tuxedos."

There is no reason why you and your company can't have similar stories. You don't have to give the farm away or go to the extreme on a daily basis. You just need to actively consider your customer's happiness and satisfaction and then give them a little more than what they are expecting.

It's time to stand up to the fear of mediocrity and become the company that stands proudly behind its products by honoring its word. Provide great products, amazing service, and give a KILLER Guarantee (whatever it may be) and you will win! It's really that simple. We guarantee it!

Chapter 8

The Power of Social Proof

"Are you serious? You're telling me that you haven't seen the movie 'Inception?' Have you been living under a rock or what? Dude, you have got to go see it! It's one of my favorite movies ever!"

Or how about this one...

"Hey man, we went and tried that new Chinese restaurant over on Main Street and it was the worst food we've ever had. It looked like the food had been sitting out on the table for days, so we ended up eating jello and animal crackers. Whatever you do, avoid that place like the plague!"

More than likely, you have either praised or complained about businesses similar to the examples given above. Conversations like these happen several times a day on a variety of topics, from food, to clothing, to entertainment, to pretty much every topic worthy of someone's opinion.

These conversations boil down to a concept called 'word of mouth advertising.' Whether we realize it or not, our perception of reality is heavily influenced by the opinions and recommendations of other people.

Odds are that you watched a movie lately because someone recommended it. Odds are that you bought a particular type of phone or went with a specific carrier because someone told you how good it was. Odds are that you ate at a restaurant recently because someone told you that they loved the food there. These are all types of word of mouth advertising and they can be incredibly powerful.

In fact, word of mouth advertising is the most powerful type of advertising on earth. It has been shaping and molding people's opinions since the first caveman who figured out how to cook meat recommended it to his Neanderthal pals.

One of the concepts closely associated with word of mouth advertising is a concept called social proof. Where word of mouth advertising is typically a one-on-one recommendation from a friend or peer, social proof is a recommendation from a group of people.

For example, have you ever seen a toothpaste commercial where they say that 9 out of 10 dentists recommend a particular brand? Or how about back in the day when Pepsi did the Pepsi Challenge commercials where they showed person after person choosing Pepsi over Coke? Or have you ever driven past a popular club and saw a line out the door and thought to yourself, "Man, that place must be really popular. We need to go there."

These are all examples of social proof and they can be just as powerful as word of mouth advertising. The great thing about social proof is that website owners can use it online as a marketing tool to create a greater demand for their products and services.

The concept behind social proof is that whether we like it or not, most people tend to follow the crowd. After all, it feels safer to be part of something big, and it's typically uncomfortable to be different, or at least significantly different than everyone else. When we see a group of people doing something, we generally assume that they are doing it for a good reason, and so we feel a compulsion to do the same.

This can be good or bad. A sale at Toys R Us – good. A run on the bank – bad. Buying that toothpaste that all those dentists recommended – good. Deciding to buy Pepsi over Coke – bad. Very bad. :-)

As with most types of data, social proof can be manipulated. For example, why didn't Pepsi show all the people that chose Coke in their taste test commercials? And, with which toothpaste did the 9 dentists compare the toothpaste that they recommended. Was it the cheap, generic, third-world-country brand or a similar competing brand?

Perhaps the biggest reason why clubs have long lines is because the outside workers who check IDs are told to take a long time deciding whether or not to let people in so that the line will stay long and other passers-by will think that the place is popular. Of course the club could afford to have five more workers checking IDs that would get everyone inside fast. But doing so would ruin the illusion that the club is in high demand for those people still deciding where to spend their night.

In the marketing world, this happens all the time. Masses of consumers are influenced by it every day for better or for worse. And whether we like it or not, social proof works nearly 100% of the time which is why it's so powerful and why it's here to stay.

Fortunately, there is one way of collecting social proof, especially online, that carries considerably more reliability and credibility than collecting and displaying the data yourself. It involves hiring an independent 3rd party. Online, these businesses are called customer rating and review services.

Customer rating and review services are provided by companies that collect ratings and reviews from your customers on your behalf and then actively display those ratings and reviews on your website for new potential customers to see. The social proof power comes with the fact that a 3rd party is gathering and displaying the ratings and reviews. When it comes to choosing a quality and effective customer rating and review service, it is important to be familiar with some of the different types of review services available...

- Some services collect ratings and reviews from all website visitors and customers while others only collect ratings and reviews from customers after they have made a purchase.

- Some services offer a short, one question survey while others ask several questions.

- Some services are easy to set up, while others take days or weeks to integrate.

- Some services are product specific, while others are based on the customer's experience as a whole.

- Some services are completely unbiased and customer driven while others risk influencing the results by using incentives such as contests and free gifts to collect feedback.

- Some services provide customer resolution options while others do not.

Here's a list of most of the companies that provide customer rating and review services; on the market today...

- bizrate.com
- powerreviews.com
- shopperapproved.com
- shopping.com
- ratepoint.com
- resellerratings.com

As we mentioned above, each of these services has different features and characteristics, and we recommend that you take the time to research each of these companies for yourself.

Here is an example of the power of social proof, particularly as it relates to customer ratings and reviews.

Have you ever heard of a little company called amazon.com?

If you were to go to amazon.com and do a search for any product, you would find that nearly half of all the content on any of their product pages are made up of customer ratings and reviews. Half the content!

Take their #1 selling product, the Amazon Kindle. If you look at the Kindle webpage, you will see several types of built-in social proof:

- They have video testimonials of customers who use it.

- They have written customer testimonials that are quoted in the content section.

- There's a cumulative ratings chart to give you a quick, overall idea of what most customers think about the Kindle.

- There are in-depth reviews from some of amazon.com's clients that use the Kindle.

- They even add customer ratings in front of the price of other complimentary products and accessories on the page!

The Reviews Are In

"The new Kindle is the best e-reader $100 (or less!) can buy." - **Engadget**

"... if what you want is pure e-reading pleasure for the lowest price around, this is a big, definite winner." - **GigaOm**

"The new Amazon Kindle rings in at a bargain $79 price, establishes the new class standard for affordable ebook readers, and still features the best ebook store on the market." - **PC Mag**

"I can't think of a single other gadget that costs less than $100 that I'd actually recommend, which makes the new Kindle just about the best Christmas gift out there." - **Popular Science**

"The basic Kindle e-reader from Amazon now starts at $79, a price point that's very hard to resist. It seems that those of us late-adopters who have hung back will be nicely rewarded for our patience and circumspection." - **Chicago Tribune**

And that's just one page in Amazon! Every product page in Amazon is just like this one. Why? Because they know that customer ratings and reviews SELL! In fact, customer ratings and reviews are amazon.com's #1 sales strategy.

It is logical to believe that if the largest, most successful online store of all time continues to consistently use social proof for half of all the content on their website, then it's probably working for them. Anyone in the ecommerce business should follow their example.

Unfortunately, Amazon doesn't sell their rating and review software. But fortunately, one of the rating and review services we mentioned above has several of the characteristics and features of Amazon's system.

The company we highly recommend is Shopper Approved.

We recommend Shopper Approved for several reasons...

1) Instead of focusing on product ratings and reviews, Shopper Approved focuses on Customer Feedback Reviews, or in other words, what customers thought about their shopping experience as a whole.

There are several benefits to this approach, but here are just a few of the main reasons why it's better to collect customer feedback reviews instead of product reviews...

- The reviews are a lot easier to collect. In fact, Shopper Approved clients get 43% of their customers to leave ratings and reviews after they buy.

- They are way easier to integrate into your website. It takes less than five minutes to set up compared to several, if not dozens of hours with product reviews.

What's your score? - www.TrustFactorBook.com/score

- They are a lot more flexible. Typically a product review is only valuable on the actual product page for which the review was written for, but customer feedback reviews can be added anywhere, on any page, making them much more valuable.

- They generate higher positive ratings. In fact, if you were to add up the number of 4 and 5-star ratings that Amazon's #1 selling Kindle gets for example, it equals 83%. But Shopper Approved pulls over 94% 4 and 5-star ratings on average across hundreds of different websites.

- They generate lower negative ratings. For example, if you look at the amount of 1-stars that the Kindle gets, you'll find that 8.1% of everyone that buys it actually hates it! But with Shopper Approved, less than 1 half of 1 percent ever rate a 1-star, and again that's on average across hundreds of websites. Just to put this into perspective, that works out to a single 1-star rating for every 200 orders, compared to 16 1-star ratings out of every 200 Kindle orders.

2) Shopper Approved has a built-in customer resolution system that automatically attempts to resolve any concerns while the customer is still filling out their review.

First, Shopper Approved alerts the business that a customer has a problem. Without gathering feedback, how would you ever know if a customer has an issue unless they contact you directly? This approach gives business owners a fast, accurate assessment of the issue, providing a unique opportunity to WOW! the customer.

Second, it opens an exclusive two-way communication channel between the customer and the business owner. If a customer has a problem, the business can simply contact the customer and help them resolve any issues before the issue escalates, creating a win-win relationship.

Third, once the customer's issue is resolved, the customer is given the ability to re-rate the company and provide a higher rating!

3) Shopper Approved never uses gimmicks like contests or free gifts to gather ratings like other companies do.

4) Shopper Approved is completely automated, which means that you can just let it run in the background and it will collect your customer's ratings and reviews. It has email alert options that you can set to inform you of any issues that customers might have.

Regardless of which customer rating and review service you end up using, any of them are a thousand times better than the alternative of gathering customer reviews manually. Think of how much time and hassle it takes to just get one review from one customer the traditional way...

First of all you have to directly contact your customer, which means that you either have to write him an email or make a phone call.

Then you have to ask him if he had a good experience with his order.

Then you have to ask him if he would be willing to take some time and give you a review. If he says no, then you have to start all over.

Then you have to wait and hope that he actually does it. If not, then you either have to keep bugging him, or you guessed it, go back and start over.

Once you finally get the review, then you have to format it.

What's your score? - www.TrustFactorBook.com/score

Then you have to figure out where you're going to actually put it on your website.

Then you have to go into the html code and manually add it to your website.

Then you have to check it to make sure that it looks right and it loaded up properly.

Wow! That's a lot of work!

We know because this is how we used to collect customer reviews and it was a huge pain. But now we use customer rating and review software, and it's literally like going from the ice ages to the 21st century overnight.

One thing we love about social proof, especially online, is that once you have it you can leverage it over and over again. As long as you keep making sales, customer rating and review software keeps collecting statistics. Over time, the amount of social proof will multiply and your company will continue to be more attractive and increasingly compelling to new customers.

If you're serious about competing online these days, you have to have an edge. You have to have something that customers can instantly relate to and associate with, and time and again history has shown us that people trust people. Adding customer rating and review software to your website, along with displaying customer feedback seals and testimonials on your website, will give you that unique personal touch that your customers want, which will be the motivating force behind getting them to buy from you.

Chapter 9

Bonus Strategy – The Relationship

You've probably heard the saying "It's not what you know, it's who you know." This phrase is often used to describe the ability that a person has to leverage something that they have of value through someone else they know and with whom they have a relationship of trust. After all, if there's no mutual trust and respect in a relationship, then there is no relationship.

What we mean by this is that your success depends on how much people trust you - not just that they simply know you. You must create a trusting relationship with those around you and more especially with those in your market.

Building a relationship can mean the difference between closing a sale and losing it to your competitor. The best way for you to create and build an ongoing relationship with your prospects and customers is to differentiate yourself and your company by becoming someone that they look to and trust for information and advice.

When you take a look at the average Joe on the street, you may think that there is nothing unique about him until he does something out of the ordinary, like step up to a podium and start talking about a specialized subject with confidence and experience. Suddenly he becomes an expert (remember that perception is reality) – a trusted authority that people look up to and admire. Suddenly his opinions matter and people start taking action based on his suggestions.

Bottom line: If you want a greater chance of building a solid, ongoing relationship of trust with your customers, you need establish yourself as a credible, trusted authority in your market.

What's your score? - www.TrustFactorBook.com/score

Here are a few tips on establishing credibility:

- **Talk about your experiences online and offline.** If you have successfully run an offline business, use your experiences to establish your credibility as a business builder. If you've been in sales and marketing before, use what you have learned to establish your credibility as a copywriter, for example.

- **Show proof that you (and your company) are the authority.** Share photos, screen shots, videos and any form of proof that gives the impression and perception that you know what you are doing. For example, you can display photos of you with other experts, or videos of you on stage or doing something that would show others that you are the expert.

- **Write a book (or ebook).** Few things lend a professional more credibility than authorship. Whether it is a book, system, specialized product or a unique way of thinking, the key is to do something spectacular in your field or market. Potential customers and even competitors will appreciate and respect you for your contribution.

- **Let others tell the story.** It is often better to let others sing your praises – especially in the form of testimonials and endorsements. The key is to do something creative and then have others tell the world how wonderful you are.

One thing to keep in mind is the word 'building' in the phrase building a relationship of trust. It usually takes time to establish credibility and trust with a customer, which means that you have to try and engage them through more than one type of medium. With that in mind, here are ten ways that you can keep your prospects interest while building an interactive relationship with your customers:

- Email Marketing
- Webinars
- Teleseminars
- Social Media
- Direct Mail
- Magazine
- Podcasts
- Applications
- Live Streaming Video
- Live Events

In this chapter we'll explain how to use these ten mediums in your business. You will need to decide which of these methods to use based on which will work best for you and your business. You don't have to implement all of these strategies, but we do suggest that you apply at least two.

EMAIL MARKETING

Let's take a look at why email marketing is so effective when building relationships.

- **Email marketing is highly scalable.** By composing an email and customizing it to suit the reader, with the click of a button you can reach thousands of people instantly! Unlike an 'offline' business where the more customers you have, the busier you are, in email marketing, it is much easier because regardless of the size of your mailing list, whether it is 100 or 10,000, your entire email list gets notified – all with the same amount of effort!

- **Email marketing is personal.** Auto-responders allow you to customize the emails, allowing you to connect with the subscriber individually. The more personalized your email, the better the result (so treat it as though you are writing to your best friend).

- **You can automate many tasks with your auto-responder.** For every new opt-in subscriber, you can schedule your emails, building a unique relationship with them. You can choose what to send to them, when to send it to them and the frequency between each email.

- **Email marketing acts as a good pre-sell.** You might not be able to cram a sales letter into your email, but at least you can pre-sell your subscriber and lead a subscriber to your blog, sales letter or website to check out what you have to offer. Test out different ways that will put them in the right frame of mind before they evaluate what you have to offer.

- **Email also works well to sell add-ons and upgrades.** Once they have purchased the product and they like it, there is a good chance they'll be interested in more of your products.

Whether you are emailing you clients daily, weekly, or monthly, it is essential to understand that giving value is essential to building a strong relationship.

Here are some tips on cultivating a meaningful, professional relationship with your subscriber:

- **Keep in touch with your mailing list often.** Don't mail them only when you need to promote a product. Let them know when something memorable happens, like an employee who had triplets, or a customer who turned 90, or funny video your friend made. Keep in touch with your subscribers so they will remember you. Not doing so will severely damage any chance of a long-term relationship.

- **Ask about their needs and concerns.** Use surveys and questionnaires to get them involved. Ask them what they want you to provide in order to help them with their problems. If they participate, heed their advice if at all possible, then send them a free gift or a significant discount on their next purchase.

- **Send them gifts sometimes.** It could be in the form of free reports, blog articles, videos or even free membership access! Make sure you don't trick them into offering something at a discount if you say it is free. Make these freebees valuable and they will look forward to future correspondence.

- **Be personal.** Let them see your human side or your personal life. Make videos of yourself and your team. Include the bloopers.

- **Be educational.** When you impart something of value to your subscribers, they will see you as a teacher and listen to what you say.

If you are not currently building an email list of subscribers, now is the time. Here are the top 5 email auto-responders that we suggest:

iContact.com
Aweber.com
Infusionsoft.com
Constantcontact.com
Getresponse.com

One last thing when it comes to email marketing:

- **Don't worry about subscribers unsubscribing.** This is just part of engaging people. There will always be people who unsubscribe - don't beat yourself up over it. However, there is a point when too many subscribers are unsubscribing (ie. over 0.5% opt-out rate) where you might want to analyze your emails and make sure that you are providing relevant content to your subscribers.

WEBINARS

Webinars are becoming more relevant and more mainstream than ever before. With technology improving and internet speeds increasing, it is now easier than ever to produce and deliver powerful webinars.

A webinar is an amazing way to engage your prospects, subscribers and customers. They can hear your voice, see your presentation and feel a part of a community all at one time.

Here are 5 tips to putting on a great webinar:

Organize – You must plan and organize a productive webinar well in advance of the actual event. Not preparing for the webinar will result in frustrated participants.

Prepare – Get your registrants excited to register and attend the webinar. Be specific with the webinar's content and what the audience will be learning. Make sure you give it a catchy title with the bullet points of what will be learned.

Engage – Plan on engaging your attendees with interesting and valuable information. You must keep the attention of the participants so they don't leave the webinar.

Teach – You need to provide content that informs the audience of ways to improve their lives or businesses. You cannot simply sell; a webinar should be a learning environment.

Follow-up - Schedule your webinar when the greatest number of people can attend. It is very important that you remind the registrant of the upcoming event via email, text message or any other form of communication. The key is to get them to attend. One way to provide exceptional service would be to give them a link of a replay of the webinar that they can use at their discretion.

Here are the top 7 current webinar software services we recommend:

Gotowebinar.com
Webex.com
Megameeting.com
Fuzemeeting.com
Adobe Connect 8
Microsoft Office Live Meeting
Skype (for small groups)

You can also offer pre-recorded webinar events. This is where you pre-record your webinar and essentially replay it over and over again. To the registrant, however, it looks like it is live. We suggest Automated Webinar Generator at yourwebinarevent.com/software to run your pre-recorded webinars.

TELESEMINARS

A teleseminar is much like a webinar but it is all audio and no video. It is usually over a phone line where the presenter talks for a certain amount of time on a specific topic. The same rules apply to teleseminars as they do for webinars. The key is to get the registrants to remember that you will be having the call and getting them to join at the correct time. You can also send the replay once you are finished, just remember to record it before you start.

When it comes to teleseminars, the go-to person and hands-down authority is Alex Mandossian. Go to TeleseminarSecrets.com to learn more.

SOCIAL MEDIA

We could write multiple books on the subject of Social Media. In fact, there have been many books already written. The problem with Social Media is that it is constantly changing and will continue to do so as technology and society evolve.

Here are our five rules to social marketing success:

Be consistent
Be authentic
Be conversational
Be informative
Be engaging

Here is the "Don't Be" list:

Don't be all about the numbers
Don't be salesy (we know this isn't a word but you know what we mean)
Don't be fake (people can see right through you)
Don't be impolite
Don't spam
Don't give up

Social media can be one of your most valuable tools to building relationships with your prospects and customers if you do it correctly. The key is to stay consistent and to give massive value. Trying to sell something online can be difficult, but trying to build a valuable relationship is simple. You must give, give, give and then give some more.

One last thing. Don't worry about how many followers, friends, or whatever it's called that you have on any given social channel. You could have millions of followers that could care less about what you are saying. Or you could have 100 followers that devour every word you create. Now that's leverage!

DIRECT MAIL

This is something that we are implementing in our business that we believe is going to create the WOW factor. Imagine everyone who buys a product or service from you getting a surprise valuable gift mailed to their home or place of business. For example, suppose we sent all of our customers this book in the mail. Do you think that would build upon an already great relationship, even if they don't read it? Sure it will.

Even if you simply send a post card in the mail thanking your customer for their purchase you will create the WOW factor. You won't necessarily see the ROI right away, but your relationship with your new customer will begin to improve!

Sendoutcards is a company that we like to use for sending cards and post cards to build relationships. They allow you to pick out a card, write a note and provide an address all online. Then they print the card, put a stamp on it, and mail it for you. You can check them out at Sendoutcards.com/6108.

MAGAZINES

A powerful way to influence and create rapport is by creating a magazine for your followers. The easiest and most affordable way of doing this is by creating an online magazine, sometimes called an ezine. You must be consistent (we suggest a quarterly magazine) in the creation and distribution, whether you print or email your magazine. You also must send valuable information in each issue or you will be wasting your time and your reader's time.

The way to make the creation process easy is by inviting industry experts to write articles for your magazine. This frees up you and/or your staff from having to write all the articles and provides different views and perspectives.

The magazine can eventually become a revenue source by selling advertising. But we suggest you do this sparingly. Remember that the magazine is a tool for creating relationships with your followers and for delivering valuable content.

PODCASTS

Some people don't like to be in front of the video camera. For them, podcasting can be an amazing tool for reaching their audience. Podcasting is online audio content that is delivered by an RSS feed. A good example of this is iTunes, which is essentially an RSS feed of audio shows or content.

Think of podcasting as just another way of reaching your audience. Some people love to listen to their mp3 players while they're exercising, driving, etc. This is a perfect time for them to listen to your podcast.

APPLICATIONS

There are many forms of applications that allow you to engage an audience. Here are just a few examples:

- Mobile applications
- Desktop applications
- Social Media applications
- Browser applications

With an application, you have the ability to send your message quickly and efficiently to grab the attention of your subscribers. There are really no set rules to creating an application, just keep in mind that it becomes a channel that you must consistently manage in order to remain effective.

LIVE STREAMING VIDEOS (Webcasts)

Webcasts are becoming more popular than ever due to services like Ustream.tv and Livestream.com. This can take a bit more technological know-how, but it is becoming easier to use every year. Webcasts allow you to create a TV show that gives you the opportunity to talk about whatever you would like for however long you want. They are extremely powerful!

LIVE EVENTS

In almost every case, there is nothing better than meeting people face to face. This is why live events are one of the most effective ways of building valuable relationships with your market. Live events however can be expensive and usually take a significant amount of time and planning to successfully pull off.

Meetup.com can be a good start to creating a live event in your local area. A live event must be well organized and worth someone taking time out of their lives to attend. The rewards are often worth the effort for those that have the ability and charisma to see them through.

There they are: ten ways to build quality relationships while keeping in contact with your prospects and customers. We want to emphasize that you do not have to apply all ten of these methods right away to be successful. What we do want you to do is to pick at least two that resonate with your message, product and company and then DO THEM CONSISTENTLY!

Chapter 10

The Three C's

To be truly successful in business and in life, we believe that there are three main areas of focus. We call them the Three C's.

- Be Conscious
- Be Committed
- Be Consistent

These principles are not new by any means, but they are essential!

Be CONSCIOUS

Successful people are conscious about every aspect of their lives, whether physical, mental, spiritual, or relational. Unsuccessful people are simply letting life take them wherever it happens to take them. This opposes our definition of conscious living.

When you are conscious, you are aware of the direction you are heading in life, and you are moving forward. When you're unaware of where you're going, you simply cannot progress. To be conscious, you have to be constantly aware of what you want, why you want it, and how you are going to achieve it – whatever the 'it' might be.

One thing that we do regularly in our business to stay conscious is to go on Power Walks. A power walk is just a walk that you go on to help you clear your mind to better visualize where you have been, where you are and where you're going.

During a power walk, we recommend that you do 3 things:

1) Say a prayer of gratitude. This is a great way to kick off a power walk because it helps to put your thoughts and ambitions in a humble state of peace and clarity. This will open your thoughts to ideas and possibilities that you normally would not have the time or patience to consider and contemplate.

2) Review your main goals. Every successful person has goals. Ironically, only a small fraction of the population actually write down their goals. Various studies have shown that in many cases, people are much more likely to be successful if they actually write their goals down. Once you've said your prayer of gratitude, go over your main goals in your head. Think about where you are at in your process of achieving those goals and where you want to be. This will help you to continually reinforce your priorities and invent new and innovative ways to making your goals become a reality.

3) Once you've reviewed your main goal (or goals), come up with something you can do today that will move you one-step closer to obtaining them. It might be as simple as a phone call or an email, or it could be writing a card to the CEO with whom you want to work or partner.

Power walks will help you feel rejuvenated, refreshed and ready to take on new challenges and reach new levels of success!

Remember, that in order to desire anything, you first must be conscious of that desire. Then you must create inside and outside of you an awareness of what it is that you need to do to accomplish the specific desire. Your mindset is at least 90% of your success and the rest simply follows.

With regards to this book and your success online, you must be mindful of your market, your prospect and especially your customer. Be conscious of what they want and need and their respect and trust toward you and your company will follow.

Be COMMITTED

Just because someone is conscious about something doesn't mean that he or she is going to take any action. For example, a very high percentage of adults in the United States are overweight and I guarantee you that most people are aware and conscious, but that doesn't mean they are doing anything about it. Therefore, being conscious is the starting point; commitment is the next step to success.

Now that you are conscious, you have an obligation to stay committed to what it is you want. You must commit yourself and your company to achieving your goals. We could write a whole course just on commitment, but obviously that is not the purpose of this book. Just keep in mind that commitment, much like faith, is something that comes from within. No one can give it to you. Commitment is a learned talent. Being committed means you will do whatever it takes, overcoming any obstacle to achieve your goal. It means that you will never give up.

We mentioned goals in the Be CONSCIOUS section above. Goals are a huge part of staying focused and committed. In order to help you create effective goals, we are including an effective 5-step process to writing effective goals and reaching them:

1) Write down your goal (or goals) on a piece of paper or word document.

2) Underneath your goal, write down the reasons why you absolutely must accomplish your goal(s).

3) Write down the date on which you plan on reaching your goal(s).

4) Sign and date the goal

5) Keep the goal in front of you – put it where you will see it everyday and not forget about it.

The reason this format is so effective is because you are, in effect, writing up a personal contract. As we all know, a contract is a legally binding document, so by signing and dating your goals, you are in essence entering into a formal agreement with yourself. And as soon as you sign it, human nature is to naturally start thinking about how you're going to fulfill it.

Talk to anyone that has accomplished a significant feat such as earning a million dollars, or running a successful online business and they will tell you that they had specific goals and were committed.

Commit yourself and your company today to being trustworthy and transparent and you will reap the rewards of success.

Be CONSISTENT

Consistent, conscious, committed effort is what makes a good company great. Everyday is the day to stay conscious and committed.

Consistency means that you will persevere to the end. This doesn't mean that there won't be any bumps along the way. It just means that you will have the drive and determination to continue on the path that will take you where you want to go.

Be consistent in your marketing and you will make more sales. Be consistent with your customer service and your customers will love you and tell their friends.
Be consistent in building quality relationships and you will earn more profit.
Be consistent with your message and you will attract more followers.
Be consistent and honest with yourself and you will find joy.

Be Conscious, Be Committed and Be Consistent!

In this book we have covered a variety of key elements that will help you increase customer TRUST in your online business for many years to come. We hope that you've enjoyed learning about the 7 strategies to converting your online visitors into lifetime, loyal customers.

Here is just a quick review of those 7 secrets:

- Perception is Reality (Website Design)
- The Art of Transparency (Customer Service)
- Who are you - Really? (Business Verification)
- Private Parts (Privacy & Terms of Service Policies)
- Security is King (SSL & PCI Compliance)
- We 'Guarantee' you'll love this (Killer Guarantee)
- The Power of Social Proof (Customer Reviews)
- Bonus Strategy – The Relationship (Establishing Authority)

Now it is time to get serious. Sit down and evaluate your business to find out if you are doing everything possible to build TRUST and credibility online. To help you, we've created some thought provoking questions below.

As you read these questions, seriously ponder their implications from your customer's point of view, because understanding their point of view makes all the difference in the level of success of your business.

Does my website <u>look</u> like a million bucks?

How do people perceive me and my business when they visit my website?

What's your score? - www.TrustFactorBook.com/score

Do I have at least a phone number, email address (support ticket system) and a physical address visible or easily accessible on every page of my website?

Am I doing everything possible to give my customers an amazing experience with my customer service?

Is my business identity verified by a reliable 3rd party?

Do my customers have a simple, effective way to resolve unexpected problems or issues?

Is my Privacy Policy and Terms of Service agreement easily accessible on my website?

Do I have an SSL installed on my website? Do I get a PCI scan at least quarterly to protect my site from hackers?

Have I created a Killer Guarantee that gives my customers warm fuzzy feelings as they buy?

Am I gathering customer ratings and reviews? Have I integrated social proof into my website?

What am I doing to continue to build my relationship with my customers?

How did you do with the questions above? Does your business have THE TRUST FACTOR or are you just hoping to squeak by without the essentials? It's time to start pondering specific actions you can perform to improve your life and your business. If you are already having some success, now is the time to go even further and really WOW your prospects and customers by using what you've learned to take your business to the next level.

Let's face it, you spend heaps of time, money and resources getting traffic to your website. They finally get there and most of them leave without buying your product or service because you don't have the proper 'trust' tools in place to make them feel safe.

If you have a competitor in your market that is tearing it up, I would bet you that they are going the extra mile. They're probably doing many if not all of the strategies discussed in this book and you need to catch up to them and then surpass them if you want to stay in business. This might sound harsh, but it is the truth. This book is your official wake-up call. You need to understand the importance of building lasting, strong relationships with your customers online! These steps and strategies are incredibly simple. So don't let another person leave your website 'empty-handed' because of a lack of trust.

If you truly 'get' the trust factor, and actively implement the 7 trust strategies we've taught you in this book, we guarantee that more customers will trust you and more customers will buy from you.

Good luck!

Garrett Pierson and Scott Brandley

What's Your Score?

Visit TrustFactorBook.com/Score today
to find out your
'Trust Factor' score!

Scan above or type this URL
into your browser –
TrustFactorBook.com/Score

About The Authors

Garrett Pierson has been helping individuals and businesses find "what it takes to be successful" in creating the life they deserve and business they desire by giving them the tools and techniques to make it happen.

He is founder of **New Generation Consulting, a consulting firm** specializing in search engine optimization, social media, website conversion, and online success. Clients include Alex Mandossian, Global Marketing Strategies, Webstarget, and many more.

Garrett is author of the book **"What Success Takes"**, a print and audio book on "The Die Hard Principles of True Victory in Life, Business, and Soul." This book includes 30 interviews of successful people such as *Raymond Aaron, Mike Filsaime, Carolyn Ellis, Noah St. John, Joel Comm, Russell Brunson and many more.*

Garrett is a family centered entrepreneur that lives his passion each and every day, and it's his goal to help others do the same.

Scott Brandley has been actively selling innovative products and services online for over 14 years. Since co-founding **Trust Guard** in 2006, Scott has helped thousands of website owners build trust and credibility online by providing them with state-of-the-art PCI Vulnerability Scanning solutions, along with 3rd party Security, Business and Privacy verification services.

In 2010, Scott & Garrett successfully launched **Shopper Approved**, a fully-automated customer rating and review service that helps website owners to create huge amounts of positive social proof to help influence, educate, and motivate new customers to buy. They hit another home run in 2011 with the launch of **Rhino Support**, a web-based customer support management system for online businesses.

In addition to helping website owners improve their businesses, Scott enjoys spending time with his family, and is also very passionate about health and fitness. Both Scott and Garrett are co-founders of UtahRunning.com and RunUtah.com Magazine – two of the most influential running resources in the State of Utah.

What's your score? - www.TrustFactorBook.com/score